Branson

Branson

by

Julie Sedenko Davis

Branson (*Tourist Town Guides*®)
© 2012 by Julie Sedenko Davis
Published by: Channel Lake, Inc., P.O. Box 1771, New York, NY 10156-1771
http://www.touristtown.com

Author: Julie Sedenko Davis
Copyeditor: Phyllis Elving
Cover Design: Julianna Lee
Maps: Michael London
Page Layout Design: Mark Mullin
Publisher: Dirk Vanderwilt

Front Cover Photos:
"Hughes Brothers" © Hughes Brothers Show, Branson MO
"Wildfire Coaster" © Silver Dollar City
"Guitar" © Shutterstock
Back Cover Photo:
"Butterfly Palace" © Julie Sedenko Davis

Published in July 2012

ISBN-13: 978-1-935455-11-0

Disclaimer: The information in this book has been checked for accuracy. However, neither the publisher nor the author may be held liable for errors or omissions. *Use this book at your own risk.* To obtain the latest information, we recommend that you contact the vendors directly. If you do find an error, let us know at corrections@channellake.com.

Channel Lake, Inc. is not affiliated with the vendors mentioned in this book, and the vendors have not authorized, approved or endorsed the information contained herein. This book contains the opinions of the author, and your experience may vary.

Help Our Environment!

Even when on vacation, your responsibility to protect the environment does not end. Here are some ways you can help our planet without spoiling your fun:

★ Ask your hotel staff not to clean your towels and bed linens each day. This reduces water waste and detergent pollution.

★ Turn off the lights, heater, and/or air conditioner when you leave your hotel room.

★ Use public transportation when available. Tourist trolleys are very popular, and they are usually cheaper and easier than a car.

★ Recycle everything you can, and properly dispose of rubbish in labeled receptacles.

Tourist towns consume a lot of energy. Have fun, but don't be wasteful. Please do your part to ensure that these attractions are around for future generations to visit and enjoy.

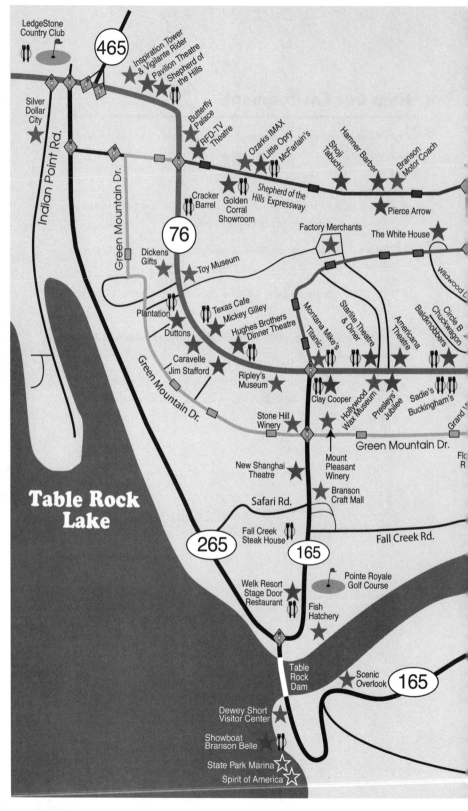

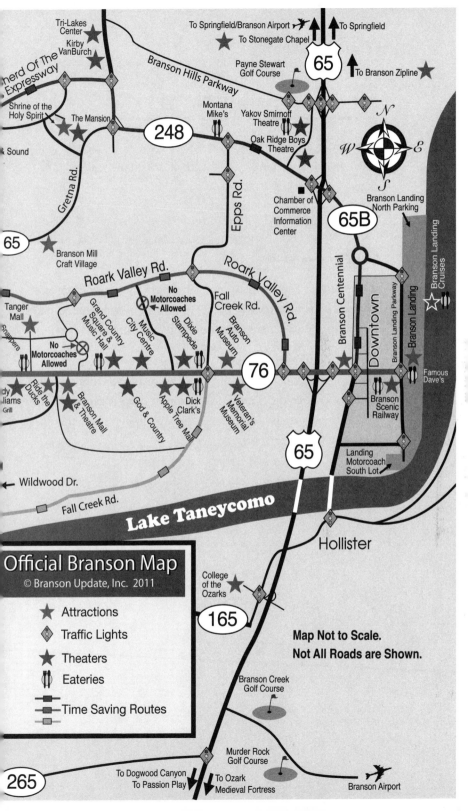

How to Use this Book

Attractions are usually listed by subject groups. Attractions may have an address, website (●), and/or telephone number (☎) listed.

Must-See Attractions: Headlining must-see attractions, or those that are otherwise iconic or defining, are designated with the ★ **Must See!** symbol.

Coverage: This book is not all-inclusive. It is comprehensive, with many different options for entertainment, dining, and shopping, but there are many establishments not listed here.

Prices: At the end of many attraction listings is a general pricing reference, indicated by dollar signs, relative to other attractions in the region. The scale is from "$" (least expensive) to "$$$" (most expensive). Contact the attraction directly for specific pricing information.

Table of Contents

Acknowledgements

Britt, thanks for your encouragement, your valuable opinions, and your sacrificial trips to the theatre lobby with our two-year-old. Most of all, thank you for being proud of me.

Nicole and Allyson, my beautiful girls, thank you for the gift of your enthusiasm every time we got to stay in another hotel (yeah!), watch another show, and try out another restaurant. Watching you laugh and play and act silly is my favorite performance of all.

To my Dad, a truly great writer, I hope this makes up for that correspondence course I never completed. Mom, thanks for always believing I was a great writer, too. Sarah Burton, thanks for teaching me about websites, turning me on to English tea, being my emergency babysitter and good friend. Cindy Merry, I am forever grateful for all of your advice, emails, phone calls, and itinerary-making on my behalf.

To the performers who make Branson an exceptional place for family entertainment: Thank you for inspiring us and investing your amazing talent in the Ozarks. Thanks to the restaurant and hotel managers, business owners, golf pros and others who opened their doors to me and answered my endless questions.

To you, the reader, thank you for trusting me for advice about your Branson getaway. I hope you will make memories as special as the ones I've made while writing this book.

For information about the author and her latest Branson discoveries, visit:

www.juliesedenko.com

Introduction

Tucked into the Ozark Mountains of southwestern Missouri, the Branson/Lakes area is a special place, unique in many ways from other vacation destinations. The town itself is home to about 7,500 residents, but in the course of a year eight million people spend some time here.

Branson is given a lot of different monikers: "an unspoiled Las Vegas," "Mayberry with a cover charge," and "America as it should be." However it's described, there is no doubt this is a town with a distinctive personality. It's a place for families to build memories in a worry-free environment and for veterans to be honored at every turn. Here in the proverbial buckle of the Bible belt, people are not hesitant to talk about their faith in God. Older folks relish the ambiance of another time.

While the atmosphere harkens to an earlier era, Branson entertainment offers the chance to experience the best talents of the past and the future all in one place. The Beatles, the Osmonds, the Eagles, Andy Williams, Roy Rogers, and the Righteous Brothers are all neighbors in Branson, in person or in tribute. Sharing the Highway 76 "Strip" with these icons are newer stars: the Duttons of *America's Got Talent*, some of the world's most talented performing families, internationally known acrobats, hilarious comedians, and world-famous magicians. Branson staples that have been here since the beginning—the Baldknobbers, the Presleys, and *The Shepherd of the Hills* outdoor drama—continue the traditions that started it all.

Today there are more than 100 performances to choose from in Branson. In fact, there are more theater seats here than on

New York City's Broadway. But in Branson, folks do more than simply see a show. They walk away feeling a sense of friendship with performers who take the time to sign autographs and get to know their guests.

Beyond the lights of the Branson Strip are three lakes framed by the beautiful mountains of the Ozarks. Camping, hiking, water sports, and world-class fishing can all be experienced here. The Lakeside Forest Wilderness Area offers cave exploration, hiking trails, and views of Lake Taneycomo. Branson hasn't forgotten the golfers, either. Award-winning courses designed by some of the top names in golf draw players of every level to Branson.

There are a few things visitors should be prepared for when visiting Branson. Veterans, be prepared to stand often, because you'll be recognized at every turn for the contributions you've made to this country. Kids, be prepared to learn who's responsible for safeguarding America's freedom, and how to honor them. Everyone, be prepared to have fun!

Area Orientation

Getting to know Branson is pretty simple as long as you have a local, color-coded map and the proper clothing to be prepared for unexpected weather changes. Special events bring unique experiences throughout the year. Branson is always changing! Shows change venues often; some close and new ones open. Be sure to check the local websites for the most current information while vacation planning.

Area
Orientation

BRANSON'S FOUR (OR FIVE) SEASONS

One of the appealing things about Branson is there are four distinct seasons: mild springs, warm summers, colorful falls, and scarf-and-mitten winters. Regardless of the season, it's a good idea to have an umbrella handy. Summer storms are common and bring a nice break from sometimes-humid conditions.

July and August are the hottest months, with temperatures climbing as high as 90° F. That may sound delightful to folks visiting from Arizona, but this is not a dry heat, which does make a bit of a sticky difference. Summer nighttime lows are usually in the 60s.

Visitors from Minnesota may describe winters here as chilly, while coastal visitors might think "bitterly cold" to be more accurate. Actual highs in January are usually in the 30's with lows averaging in the teens and 20's. Wind chill can make it feel a whole lot colder. Dress in layers, and bring gloves and scarves. It does snow, but not often, and there's usually not much accumulation. There can be ice, so caution is required.

Actually, Branson recognizes five official tourist seasons. Hot Winter Fun is Branson's name for the months of January, February, and March. This is definitely the most economical time to visit, as many shows and attractions lower their prices for the winter. The traffic is much lighter, but there are plenty of attractions open. Some performers take a winter hiatus; be sure to check show schedules. Winter is the only time to see some of Branson's favorite entertainers all together in one show. The Hot Winter Fun Big Show has featured Jim Stafford, the Hughes Brothers, Pierce Arrow, Kirby VanBurch, Tony Roi, Clay Cooper, and others. Every January brings a much-anticipated professional ice-carving competition at (where else?) the Titanic Museum. This is also a great time to go trout fishing on Lake Taneycomo; Lilley's Landing and Marina holds two catch-and-release tournaments. Check 🖱 explorebranson.com for information on these special events.

SPRING

Ozark Mountain Spring arrives in April. Temperatures are starting to warm up, and trees and flowers are beginning to bloom. Among popular spring events are the Kewpiesta, a Kewpie doll festival, and Plumb Nellie Days, when "plumb nearly everything goes." This long-standing tradition is held downtown in May, with contests and even a royal court; admission is free.

SUMMER

June begins the Cool Summer Fun season. Families converge on Branson, and everything is running in high gear. White Water begins its Night Water event, staying open late so patrons can enjoy the waterpark on warm summer evenings.

Car enthusiasts descend on Branson for the Super Summer Cruise held at the Shepherd of the Hills Homestead. The Fourth of July is an especially beautiful time, with spectacular fireworks at the Shepherd of the Hills, Chateau on the Lake, Big Cedar Lodge, Branson Landing, Rockaway Beach, and historic downtown Hollister.

FALL

Fall for the Ozarks, beginning in September, is arguably the prettiest time to visit. The weather is almost perfect, the landscape is colorful. This is a great time to take a drive or go on an area tour; the website ● explorebranson.com suggests routes for autumn color tours. Kids are back in school so there aren't as many little ones in the audience, but most shows are still running.

WINTER

Branson gets a head start on the holidays with its Ozark Mountain Christmas. Everything gets decked out in its seasonal best beginning November 1st. Visitors will want to head straight for Silver Dollar City theme park, recognized as one of the country's top holiday destinations. Most shows get holiday makeovers, focusing on seasonal music for the second half. A few are entirely Christmas-themed, including the Hughes Brothers, Dixie Stampede, Andy Williams, and Shoji Tabuchi. Some shows are only staged at this time of year, such as Miracle of Christmas. Shopping is a festive experience, with caroling, visits from Santa, and seasonal decorations. Branson Landing and the Grand Village malls are favorite holiday shopping destinations.

HOLIDAY EVENTS

The Christmas spirit is easy to come by in Branson. There are almost as many special events as shows to keep visitors entertained. For details on the events listed here, contact the **Branson/Lakes Area Convention and Visitors Bureau** (☎ *877.272.6766* 🖱 *explorebranson.com*).

VETERANS HOMECOMING

The season kicks off early in November with the largest veterans homecoming in the nation. A multitude of special events ends with a Veterans Day parade in downtown Branson.

BRANSON AREA FESTIVAL OF LIGHTS

A mile's worth of lights synchronized to music, this Branson tradition features 175 different displays, and more are added every year. It is open nightly, beginning at dusk to 11 p.m. and runs from November 1 to January 2. The Festival of Lights entrance is on Shepherd of the Hills Expressway across from Sight and Sound Theatre.

ADORATION PARADE AND LIGHTING CEREMONY

This downtown tradition has taken place in early December for more than 60 years. The parade begins after the lighting of a nearly 30-foot-tall nativity scene at the top of Mount Branson, overlooking Lake Taneycomo. This is a completely non-commercial event in which the community gathers to celebrate the spiritual meaning of Christmas. Meet at the corner of Main and Commercial streets for the lighting ceremony. Visit down-townbranson.org for current schedule and parade route map.

TRAIL OF LIGHTS

A favorite for many visitors, the Trail of Lights is built on what was mentioned in The Shepherd of the Hills as the "trail nobody knows how old." Driving through illuminated themed "lands," there is Santa and the elves, Frosty, a Hawaiian holiday, even a holiday in space. Other scenes tell of Jesus' birth in Bethlehem. There are over two miles of animated displays, many accompanied by music. Admission to the trail is approximately $10 per vehicle and includes a trip to the top of Inspiration Tower where the lights can be seen from above. The trail should take less than an hour but long lines on the weekend may significantly increase this time. Many visitors first attend the dinner show, Christmas on the Trail, at the Shepherd of the Hills Pavilion; trail admission is included in the price of the show. Visit ✆ theshepherdofthehills.com for the latest information.

WHITE FLIGHT AT BUTTERFLY PALACE

More than a thousand white butterflies make up this unique "Christmas meets nature" experience. In addition to the butterflies, there are living statues of angels (similar to mimes), twinkling lights, and seasonal foliage displays.

MILITARY GALA & BANQUET

Chateau on the Lake hosts this event every year in November to honor veterans, although it's not required one be a veteran to attend. The evening includes cocktails, dinner, salute, candlelight POW/MIA service, fireworks, and entertainment; call ☎ 866.481.4252 or visit ✆ bransonveteranevents.com for information. This is a dressy event, and reservations are required.

RESORT CELEBRATIONS

Area resorts go all out during the holidays. The Keeter Center at the College of the Ozarks does a Renaissance-themed Yuletide Feast, and Chateau on the Lake holds a Victorian Homecoming with bonfires, teas, music by local choirs, and breakfast with Santa. Big Cedar stages special holiday performances, offers wagon rides through its lighted property, and even has elves on hand to tuck in the kids.

POLAR EXPRESS

Christmastime brings a magical experience for families. Kids can board the Branson Scenic Railway in their pajamas to enjoy hot cocoa and a reading of The Polar Express while enjoying a real train ride . Santa pays a visit and offers a gift to each of the young riders.

NEW YEAR'S EVE

A number of performers put on special New Year's Eve shows. Some of these include Kirby VanBurch, Hamner Barber, Jim Stafford, Legends in Concert, and Acrobats of China. Some resorts also hold New Year's Eve events; those at Big Cedar and Chateau on the Lake are among the most popular.

GETTING TO BRANSON

Branson's location 11 miles north of the Arkansas border and about 40 miles south of Interstate 44 means that a third of the country can easily get here in a day's drive. Highway 65 is an easy north-south route connecting Arkansas with Springfield and Interstate 44 by way of Branson. Those traveling from the east will likely find themselves coming into town on Highway 160; the western route to Branson is Highway 76.

AREA AIRPORTS

Since the 2009 opening of the $140 million **Branson Airport** *(4000 Branson Creek Blvd.* ☎ *417.334.7813 or* ☎ *888.359.2541* ☎ *flybranson.com, Airport Code: BKG)*, visitors can fly direct into America's favorite hometown. Branson Airport is the first privately financed and operated commercial operation in the country. Travelers will appreciate its unique common use system where, regardless of what airline is being flown, check in can be done with any counter agent. Fly Branson Travel Agency is on site for travel arrangements, show tickets, and other bookings.

The 58,000-square-foot terminal reflects its rugged Ozark environment. Five sets of animal tracks guide travelers through security, representing actual critters found in the area. This is Bass Pro country, and a miniature version of the mammoth hunting and fishing store is located in the gate area. So is Famous Dave's Bar-B-Que.

The airport is less than 10 miles from downtown Branson and practically next door to the Murder Rock golf course. For those flying privately, the Branson Jet Center is nearby. Ground transportation is available with Gray Line buses. There are also shuttles, taxis, and rental cars. There is no free parking at the airport; entering the parking lot will incur a fee, although it is reasonable.

Another option is the **Springfield-Branson National Airport** *(2300 N. Airport Blvd., Springfield* ☎ *417.868.0500* ☎ *sgf-branson-*

airport.com, Airport Code: SGF), about an hour's drive north of
Branson. American, Allegiant, Delta, and United serve the
newly built facility with direct flights from 12 cities. Rental
car companies include Avis, Budget, Hertz, Enterprise, and
National. Taxi service is also available.

Alternate regional airports include **Northwest Arkansas
Regional Airport** in Bentonville, AR *(☎ 479.205.1000)*
and **Boone County Regional Airport** in Harrison, AR *(☎
870.741.6954)*. Several larger airports add a long drive but can
be less expensive options for those traveling a good distance.
Kansas City, St. Louis, and Tulsa airports are all about four to
five hours from Branson.

BUS TOURS

One of the most popular ways to visit Branson is with a
bus tour group. Visitors can score great deals on tickets by
going the group route, and it can be fun to experience shows
and attractions with friends. To choose the right tour group,
contact the **Branson/Lakes Area Chamber of Commerce**
(☎ 800.214.3661 ✆ explorebranson.com).

GETTING AROUND

Getting around is a little nuts because Branson is a small town
with a ton of tourist traffic. A number of traffic relief routes do
offer significant help but have left the town map looking like a
plate of spaghetti.

Fortunately, the maps are everywhere, and they are excellent.
Trust them. Avoid the Strip at all costs around show time. Op-
tional streets are color-coded; the red and blue routes are always

a good idea and will save from stop-and-go traffic on the Strip. If you're using a GPS device and have any trouble with "Highway 76," try "Country Music Boulevard." The Strip is referred to by both names.

TAXI/SHUTTLE SERVICES

Branson Limo Service (☎ *417.331.1316* 🖰 *bransonlimoservice.com*) has four luxury sedans, a ten-passenger super-stretch Lincoln Town Car and a 27-passenger shuttle bus with televisions and plush seating. In addition to hourly rentals, the company offers a three-hour winery tour and a holiday light tour.

Branson Yellow Cab Co. *(1972 Hwy 165, Suite J* ☎ *417.336.6769)* supplies taxi services, and family-owned **Terry's Transport, Tickets & Golf** *(190 Potential Dr., Hollister* ☎ *417.331.2821* 🖰 *ttbranson.com)* provides transportation, show tickets, tours, and golf outings and clinics. Terry's has several shuttle buses carrying up to 26 passengers and a Lexus SUV for local taxi service.

WHAT TO PACK

Leave the formal wear in the closet. Branson is decidedly "country casual." Jeans and shorts are fine at shows and attractions. Bring an umbrella, as rainstorms can occur at any time. Sweaters during the spring and fall are also important, as the nights can get chilly; layers are important during these transition months. In addition to a heavy coat, hats, scarves and gloves are good accessories to have in the winter, especially when spending considerable time outdoors, for instance, when visiting Silver Dollar City during the Christmas season.

Many visitors like to bring or buy an autograph book, while others would rather have an entertainer's signature on a show souvenir. Next to the kids, the most important thing to remember is a camera and extra batteries!

HELPFUL WEBSITES

Sorting through the seemingly endless array of Branson-related websites can seem like a daunting task. Following are a few of the more helpful sites.

● **ExploreBranson.com** This is the official website for the Branson community, the Branson/Lakes Area Chamber of Commerce, and the Convention and Visitors Bureau. In addition to attraction information, it offers coupons, specials, and even an itinerary builder. Just enter your arrival and departure dates into the appropriate field located on the home page and it will show you all of the attractions and shows (including times) available during your vacation. This feature is extremely helpful as it filters out shows you won't be able to see.

● **ShowsInBranson.com** The official website for the League of Branson Theatre Owners & Show Producers gives a rundown on Branson's shows and also includes an itinerary builder and a fan club section.

● **HalfPriceOzarks.com** This is a great place to find half-price certificates for shows, restaurants, and more. Some can be printed out on a home printer, but many are mailed, so allow plenty of time before vacation.

● **OzarkAnglers.com** This is the place to go for information on fishing in the Ozarks, including details on the three major lakes and local rivers. Regulations, water levels, and even fly recipes are posted here along with helpful articles.

VETERANS

Branson is a town that appreciates veterans, and many veterans come here for entertainment and the chance to connect with others who have served. Veterans are honored in virtually every venue. To receive a discount, be sure to tell ticket agents if you are a veteran. The same goes for restaurants, hotels, and almost any other local business. For information on the many activities, special events, and services geared toward veterans, go to the website ● bransonveterans.com or call ☎ 417.337.8387.

THINGS TO DO FOR FREE

Those on a budget can find plenty of things to do in the Branson area that won't cost a dime. The Branson Landing outdoor mall alongside Lake Taneycomo provides free entertainment to those with the self-control to stay out of the stores. Music, water fountain shows, beautiful views, and even occasional live performances are all free of charge.

Local lakes offer many free activities, including Moonshine Beach and the Shepherd of the Hills Fish Hatchery. Several wineries in and around Branson offer free tours and tasting, and the College of the Ozarks allows visitors on free tours of its campus.

Some theaters open for worship services on Sundays, and given the level of talent in Branson, they have some of the best special music anywhere. Sometimes local celebrities take the stage unannounced. The Little Opry Theatre has an Ol' Time Gospel Hour each week; call ☎ 800.419.4832 or go to ⬤ bransonimax. com/big-live-shows for times. God and Country Theatre has Cowboy Church on Sunday mornings; call ☎ 417.334.6806 or visit ⬤ gacbranson.com/CowboyChurch.

Area Orientation

History

How Branson came to be the live music capital of the world makes a fascinating story. The perseverance and character of early pioneers to the rugged Ozark wilderness was made famous by a traveling preacher whose writings forever changed this beautiful area.

EARLY HISTORY

The popular lakes of this corner of Missouri didn't exist in the area's early history. The White River was the predominant source of water and transportation, flowing through forests that looked much different than today's landscape.

The first recorded residents of the Ozarks were the Osage Indians, who dominated the region in the 17th and 18th centuries. But even the strong Osage could not prevail against the politics of the Louisiana Purchase of 1803 and the subsequent treaties that took away Indian lands, opening them to settlement.

With the influx of settlers, Taney County was formed in 1837. It was named after Supreme Court Chief Justice Roger B. Taney, who later presided during the infamous 1857 Dred Scot decision and administered the oath of office to more Presidents than any other chief justice. He married Ann Key, sister of Francis Scott Key who penned the words of our national anthem. A post office was established, leading to the town of Forsyth, now the county seat. Soon ferryboats were traveling the White River, and later stagecoaches and steam boats arrived.

CIVIL WAR ERA

The attack on the town of Forsyth on July 21, 1861, brought fighting to the area just a day after Bull Run, the first major battle of the Civil War. Missouri was on the fence when it came to choosing sides during the Civil War years. It wasn't unusual for members of the same family to wind up on different sides. A couple of important battles were fought nearby: the Battle of Wilson's Creek in Springfield and the Battle of Pea Ridge in Fayetteville, Arkansas.

The Civil War was a bloody conflict, but killings were not confined to conflicts between North and South. Guerilla fighters known as bushwhackers, with no real affiliation to either side, ravaged the area, stealing from and gunning down local men and even entire families. Alfred Bolin was an outlaw leader, and his stomping ground was where Murder Rock golf course is now located.

By the end of the Civil War, the area around present-day Branson was unrecognizable. Most buildings had been destroyed by fire, and nature was beginning to take back the land.

THE BALDKNOBBERS

In 1862 the federal government's Homestead Act offered free land to settlers, bringing a new population and a new beginning to the region. Homesteading wasn't easy in this untamed wilderness. There were floods, fires, and even a grasshopper plague that annihilated crops.

Lawlessness was a major problem. Many crimes, including murder, were being committed without punishment. Tired of the situation, a group of Taney County citizens formed a vigilante group called the Baldknobbers. The name came from the sparse tops or "bald knobs" of the Ozarks hills, which served as secret meeting places. There are many versions to the Baldknobbers history and descendents of the group still have strong convictions about what may have actually happened.

We do know there were two factions. The first group, begun in Taney County with about a dozen men, originally called themselves the "Law and Order League" or the "Citizen's Committee." It sought to curb the lawlessness and, in fact, was successful in many respects. Problems started as the group grew into the hundreds. Many believed their punishments were extremely harsh and even criminal in and of themselves. Disturbed, some of the original group stopped being associated with the Baldknobbers altogether. Others formed another passionate group called the anti-Baldknobbers. Animosity remained, even among descendents of these groups, long after the Baldknobbers disappeared from society.

While the original Taney County faction of the Baldknobbers formally disbanded in the town square at the recommendation of Missouri's Adjutant General, another faction of the group was just beginning in Christian County to the north. Some believe this is the faction that tried to keep their anonymity by donning hoods with horns and doling out the cruelest of punishments even for the most insignificant infraction. Ultimately, federal marshals put an end to the group with a trial in the town of Ozark located in Christian county. The trial resulted in the hanging of several members. The Baldknobbers era was technically over by the late 1880s although there are rumors of further rumblings as late as the 1920's.

BRANSON: MYSTERY AND MIX-UPS

Driving north or south across College Street in downtown Branson today is a history lesson that hints at intrigue, and perhaps even murder.

In 1883 Reuben Branson, a young schoolteacher from eastern Missouri, opened a combination drugstore and post office where Roark Creek and the White River met (now Lake Taneycomo). As was common, the area was named after its first postmaster: Branson.

History

The railroad began making its way into the area just after the turn of the century. Charles Fulbright, an agent for the railroad and president of the Branson Town Company, was on a mission to acquire enough land to plat the town of Branson. Fulbright had his sights set on a farm homesteaded by blacksmith Thomas Berry just south of what is now College Street, but Berry wanted to plat a town called Lucia. Before Berry was able to carry out his plans, he died unexpectedly; according to records, he hanged himself. When the job of platting the town of Lucia fell to Berry's son Henry, tragedy struck again. Henry also died unexpectedly.

In 1903 Lucia did become a recognized town, just long enough to be laid out in lots. Within two weeks the Branson Town Company owned the plat, and Lucia and Branson towns were joined. The only problem was that the lots and streets didn't quite line up. Today as you drive across College Street in downtown Branson, you can see the results of that early history: the streets still don't line up.

Reuben Branson and his wife are buried in Branson City Cemetery. Those interested in this part of the city's history can visit their gravesite.

HAROLD BELL WRIGHT

Harold Bell Wright first ventured into the Ozark hills in 1903, on his way to a climate recommended by a doctor for his failing health. But a flooded White River forced the writer-preacher to interrupt his journey. He was led to the home of John Keever Ross and his wife, Georgiana, or Anna as she was also called, with whom he stayed for the remainder of the summer.

Wright gained a deep appreciation for the Ozark landscape and people. He returned to the Ross cabin several times on subsequent visits. It was here that he wrote his novel The Shepherd of the Hills, which put Branson on the tourism map. The 1907 novel introduced readers to the beauty and the people of the area. There are various claims about the book's success—that it was second only to the Bible in sales, that it was the first novel to reach a million in sales, and so on. Whatever statistic one chooses to believe, the book was immensely popular and drew people from across the nation to see the Ozarks for themselves.

THE LAKES

In 1911 the federal government approved construction of the first hydroelectric dam west of the Mississippi. The Powersite Dam went into service in 1913 near Forsyth, impounding the waters of the White River and creating Lake Taneycomo. In 1958, Table Rock Dam was completed about six miles southwest of Branson. Branson was now a lake resort destination.

Table Rock Dam sent the frigid bottom tailwaters of Table Rock Lake into Lake Taneycomo, turning it into an environment that was perfect for trout. Taneycomo became a trout-fishing destination, while Table Rock was ideal for water sports and other types of fishing.

MODERN HISTORY

Red Foley was the first famous country singer to make his way to Branson in 1954. The chart-topping musician hosted the successful television show, Ozarks Jubilee from 1955 to 1960.

In 1959 a group of four brothers took advantage of Lake Taneycomo's popularity and began entertaining visitors on the waterfront. Bob, Jim, Lyle, and Bill Mabe had a banjo and a dobro. Their other instruments consisted of a washtub bass and, for rhythm, a washboard and the jawbone of a mule. The "Baldknobbers" were an immediate success.

The following year, the Herschend family opened Silver Dollar City theme park at the entrance to Marvel Cave. Visitors rode a Butterfield stage around the re-created pioneer town of Marmaros, saw craftsmen at work, and watched skirmishes between the Hatfields and the McCoys. The Herschends' practice of handing out silver dollars as change became an important marketing tool.

Just a few months later, the Shepherd of the Hills Outdoor Theatre presented its debut performance of the story made famous by Harold Bell Wright. At that time the theater capacity was a little over 400, compared to today's 2,000 seats.

The 1960s also brought easier access to the area with the completion of Highway 65 running north and south and

Interstate 44 going east and west. A few hotels popped up, and a few more performers began offering entertainment. In 1967 the Presleys opened the first theater on what would become famous as the Highway 76 Strip, also referred to as Country Music Boulevard. Back then it was just a roadside building with not a whole lot around it.

More attractions came, including Ride the Ducks amphibious tours in the 1970s. In 1983 Branson's first celebrity headliner, Roy Clark, opened a theater in town. More theaters followed— Hee Haw, Starlite, Musicland USA, Shoji Tabuchi, and others. The Shepherd of the Hills Inspiration Tower was erected in 1989.

In 1991, some 40 million people tuned in to watch a CBS episode of 60 Minutes about Branson. It was that show which first gave Branson the title "Live Country Music Show Capital of the Universe," resulting not only in a tourist boom but also in skyrocketing real estate sales. Big-name entertainers began to take notice. Branson offered them a chance to get off the road and enjoy a more relaxed lifestyle while continuing to perform. Ray Stevens, Jim Stafford, Mel Tillis, Buck Trent, and Boxcar Willie were among the celebrities who made a new home in Branson.

The publicity continued with an on-location airing of NBC's *Live with Regis and Kathy Lee* in 1995. That same year Dolly Parton partnered with Silver Dollar City to open the popular Dixie Stampede, and the Showboat Branson Belle began offering cruises on Table Rock Lake. Chateau on the Lake was built in 1997, the Grand Palace Theatre in 1999.

The turn of a new century brought the White Water waterpark, the Titanic Museum, Branson Landing shopping complex, and the Branson Convention Center. In 2009 the Branson Airport opened, bringing a new way for visitors to reach America's live music capital.

Silver Dollar City

(399 Silver Dollar City Pkwy ☎ 800.475.9370 📱 silverdollarcity. com) Silver Dollar City is unlike any other theme park in the nation. Built to replicate an 1880s Ozark village, it unabashedly celebrates America's heritage and traditional family values. There are thrill rides, top-of-the-line entertainment (included in the ticket price), and unique shops. Six distinct festivals are held at the park throughout the year. Silver Dollar City draws more than two million tourists annually.

HOW IT BEGAN

Silver Dollar City's beginnings can be traced back to the formation of a massive underground cave. Osage Indians are said to have discovered the cave around 1500, believing it to be a gateway to the underworld. It wasn't explored until the late 1800s, when it was dubbed Marble Cave because the walls appeared to be made of marble. (They're actually limestone.) Near the turn of the century, mining expert William Henry Lynch purchased the cave and opened it to public tours. The name was later changed to Marvel Cave to describe its enormity. Author Harold Bell Wright was a cave visitor and wrote about its beauty in *The Shepherd of the Hills*.

In 1946 Hugo and Mary Herschend, vacationing from Chicago, visited Marvel Cave and leased the property. Their idea of creating an 1880s frontier town came after visiting with a traveling salesman who had been born in Marmaros, a town once located at the entrance to the cave. Silver Dollar City opened in 1960, named for the Herschends' practice of handing out silver dollars in change.

The park's beginnings were humble: a few shops, an ice cream parlor. The McHaffie homestead and the Wilderness Church, log buildings from the 1800s, were given new life by being relocated to Silver Dollar City. As for shows, employees in costumes performed light-hearted feuds in the street, acting as the Hatfields and the McCoys. Then in 1969 the sitcom The Beverly Hillbillies filmed five episodes at Silver Dollar City, giving the budding theme park nationwide recognition. Today Silver Dollar City boasts more than 60 acres, a dozen stages, a dozen restaurants, 22 rides, 1,500 employees, and 100 resident craftsmen. The entrance to the original attraction, Marvel Cave, is located in the park's gift shop.

PARK ORIENTATION

Silver Dollar City is located just off the far west end of Highway 76 about six miles from the Branson strip. One of the best perks at the park is the free parking, with complimentary trolleys to transport visitors from the parking lot to the park's front door. Preferred and valet parking options are available for a fee.

There are a lot of hills, some of them pretty steep, within Silver Dollar City; park maps include information about the grades of hills. If you get lost, remember that if you're heading downhill you're going into the park, and if you're climbing uphill you're going toward the exit.

GENERAL INFORMATION

Silver Dollar City has an old-fashioned way of making everyone feel welcome. Those with special needs or special interests are accommodated. Any additional questions or concerns can be answered at the Guest Relations office at the park's entrance.

PERSONS WITH DISABILITIES

As a recently instituted policy, visitors who are blind, deaf. or full-time wheelchair users are admitted to Silver Dollar City free of charge. All restaurants and shops are wheelchair accessible.

DIETARY NEEDS

Prepackaged meals are available for those allergic to gluten, dairy, nuts, shellfish, or eggs. If these are not adequate, park staff will work with visitors to personalize a menu; call ☎ 800.251.5576 two to three days before your visit or email requests to foodallergy@silverdollarcity.com.

DRESS CODE

To maintain a family-friendly environment, Silver Dollar City has created a basic dress code that prohibits profane or suggestive clothing. For water rides, bathing suits may be worn by those under the age of eight, with shorts over them; anyone else wearing a swimsuit is required to wear a cover-up. Shoes with built-in wheels are not allowed in the park.

WEATHER

It often rains, even in the summer, in southwest Missouri. Sometimes it pours. Some people swarm to leave the park the minute a drop falls from the sky, but it's advisable to wait it out a bit. Often it will clear up and end in a perfect (and not so crowded) day at the park. In the meantime, check out shows, shops, restaurants, and even a few indoor rides, like Fire in the Hole and the Flooded Mine (which might be appropriate). Due to safety restrictions many rides cannot operate in colder temperatures. Some roller coasters will not run when the temperature dips below 40 degrees.

SHOW LOVER'S PASS

If shows are the main thing you want to do at Silver Dollar City, consider purchasing a Show Lover's Pass. The price is reasonable, the pass guarantees the best seats, and the ability to bypass lines. Since VIP seating is limited, it's recommended to purchase the pass online and print a voucher at home. Take the voucher to the Show Lover's Booth across from Eva & Delilah's Bakery.

TRAILBLAZER'S PASS

If rides are a priority and it's a busy day, this pass will put you at the front of the line for up to six rides. The passes are only available on select dates, and the number of passes issued each day is limited. Buy them at the Show Lover's Pass Booth across from Eva & Delilah's Bakery. Be sure to check the list of rides for which these passes are intended.

VISITING WITH BABIES AND CHILDREN

For those with young kids, the first stop should be the official ride-measuring station in The Grand Exposition. Each child is given a wristband on which parents can write their cell phone number in case of separation. This is also where children are measured to see which rides they can experience, alone or with an adult. Their wristband will allow them entry onto the appropriate attractions without needing to be measured again.

Strollers, both single and double, can be rented near the park entrance. Any restaurant (not concession stands) will provide warm water for bottles free of charge.

In addition, kids four and under eat for free at Molly's Mill. Nursing mothers will appreciate the park's four nursing stations. Two of them are large with rocking chairs and changing tables. One is located next to the Red Gold Heritage Hall. Another is near the Giant Swing. Smaller nursing stations can be found near the restrooms at Geyser Gulch and in the back of the women's restroom in the Hospitality House.

MOMS BLOG

There is an extremely helpful blog at ● silverdollarcityblog. com that lets you link to Facebook and ask seasoned moms questions about the park. This is a good place to find out what other moms say about rides, restaurants, and things to do at Silver Dollar City.

FESTIVALS

Six festivals with distinct themes are held at Silver Dollar City throughout the year, each of them featuring special entertainment, food, and activities.

WORLD FEST

World Fest begins in early April and usually lasts about a month. This festival is all about the variety of cultures and customs throughout the world. Past performances have included balancing monks from China, acrobats from Kenya,

Trinidad drummers and fire limbo dancers, the Watoto Children's Choir, Mexican dancers, and Italian flag throwers.

The Frisco Barn offers enlightenment for the taste buds with food from Ireland, Mexico, Italy, France, Greece, Germany, Asia, Latin America, and more. Visitors can learn how to create international dishes by taking classes at Silver Dollar City's Culinary & Craft School.

BLUE GRASS AND BBQ

Held in May, this festival is exactly what it sounds like. Visitors hear top performers and taste the diversity of barbecue flavors from every corner of America. The Red Gold Heritage Hall becomes the House of BBQ, complete with a nine-foot wood-fired smoker that prepares slow-cooked ribs, chicken, brisket, and pulled pork.

NATIONAL KIDS FEST

Scheduled smack in the middle of summer, Kids Fest gives youngsters plenty of opportunities to use up extra energy. The Kids Concoctions Activity Center is a favorite spot for creativity and exploration. Stunt dogs, magicians, mad scientists, VeggieTales, a Swedish rhythm band, the JEERK show, and even an ice circus have been popular performances at past festivals.

Kids will appreciate the food choices geared for the younger palette, such as a pizza buffet, hot diggety dogs, chicken crunchers, fruit cups, fries, and smoothies. Snow cones are a popular dessert, or for the competitive set (ages 12 and up), there's a banana split–eating contest.

SOUTHERN GOSPEL PICNIC

Dubbed America's biggest southern gospel picnic, this is a time of great music and food. Along with plenty of traditional quartet groups, you will hear bluegrass and country—every

kind of southern gospel—during this short festival beginning at the end of August . Award-winning recording artists like the Kingsmen, Gold City, Jeff & Sheri Easter, and the Reggie Sadler family have been featured performers. After regular park hours there is a concert every evening in Echo Hollow.

To accompany the gospel music, Silver Dollar City cooks whip up such picnic fare as double-battered fried chicken, apple-glazed or barbecue chicken, coleslaw, and cakes.

NATIONAL HARVEST FEST

More than a hundred craftsmen descend on Silver Dollar City at the end of September for this six-week festival held during what is arguably the prettiest time of year to visit the Ozarks. Jewelry, stained glass, baskets, and pottery are just a few of the products made by hand during Harvest Fest. Fall food offerings include turkey legs, corn on the cob, ribs, chili, and skillet meals, with cobblers and hot apple dumplings for dessert.

AN OLD TIME CHRISTMAS

Just walk into the park and it's obvious why it's been called one of the best holiday light shows in America. First there's the five-story musical Christmas tree lighting up the square. Beyond that, there are four million lights decking out the old-time city. It can be very cold at night at this time of year, so bring coats, hats, and gloves, and plan to enjoy some of the best hot cocoa around. You can even load it up with marshmallows, whipped cream, even chocolate chips. Hot wassail (cider) is also available.

The annual performance of Dickens' A Christmas Carol is the park's biggest production. It includes a live band, special effects, and top-notch scenery and costumes. This show is highly recommended for everyone in the family. Another fun production is the nightly Gifts of Christmas Holiday Light Parade. The kids will likely agree that this is worth staying up for when lighted toy soldiers come to shake hands with them. It's not a long parade, but it is quite interactive.

Food served during the holiday season includes a prime rib buffet, chili, s'mores, and apple dumplings. There is even an opportunity for the family to have lunch with Santa while enjoying "Mrs. Claus'" cooking. Reservations are required for this event. Call ☎ 800.475.9370 for dates and times. Pick up a souvenir mug at any food stand throughout the park and enjoy inexpensive refills on drinks whenever you visit.

PARK ATTRACTIONS

Silver Dollar City's attractions are based on the 1880s Ozark village theme. A few of them are not included in the price of admission.

MARVEL CAVE TOURS

The cavern described by novelist Harold Bell Wright was the original attraction that became Silver Dollar City. Hour-long guided tours of the wet limestone cave leave every 30 minutes. Tours are included in the park admission price. Guests first visit the stunning Cathedral Room, America's largest cave entrance room. There are a lot of stairs to climb, so the tour is not appropriate for everyone.

Lantern Light Tours are new, allowing visitors to see the cave as early explorers did. Guides dressed in period costume tell stories about the cave's history. This is the only time visitors get to see the Mammoth Room, which hadn't been part of cave tours since the 1950s. The re-opened trail also includes the bat wall and a "Spanish ladder" dating back to 1541. The Lantern Light Tour takes an hour and a half and costs extra; kids under eight are not permitted. Make reservations at the Cave Information Desk inside the Hospitality House early in the day, as spots are limited.

CULINARY AND CRAFT SCHOOL

(⬤ sdcculinarycraftschool.com) A big part of Silver Dollar City is its emphasis on the Ozarks heritage of craftsmanship. An 1880s-style farmhouse is a showcase for handmade furniture as well as being the venue for culinary classes. Actually, even the front door is a demonstration of craftsman talent.

The farmhouse may re-create an older time, but the kitchen inside is absolutely state-of-the-art. Recipes being taught vary according to the season. There is an additional charge for the cooking lessons, and it's important to make reservations, as spots are limited.

GEYSER GULCH

Dubbed the world's largest treehouse, Geyser Gulch is the ultimate playground. With plenty of room to climb and explore, kids can shoot foam balls from the second or third story (aiming at a sibling is usually a highlight) or blast water at targets. There's even a geyser spot where youngsters can get wet as they hop around unexpected blasts of water.

HALF DOLLAR HOLLER

This recent million-dollar addition to Silver Dollar City is a welcome one for parents of young children. It's a dedicated play area for kids under the age of seven. A highlight is the return of the park's hand-carved carousel. There are also treetop funhouses, climbing nets, mini–wave swings, and lots of sand.

MCHAFFIE'S HOMESTEAD

This is as authentic as it gets. McHaffie's Homestead is an actual log cabin built in 1843 and brought to Silver Dollar City in 1960. Located on the square, it offers a hands-on look at life in the 1800s. Visitors can try out the furniture, ask questions of the homestead family, and enjoy entertainment by the Homestead Pickers. Kids can take part in storytelling with Aunt Judy and visit live animals in the barnyard.

SHOPS AT SILVER DOLLAR CITY

Silver Dollar City seems to have an infinite number of stores. Each has its own niche, but American craftsmanship is the cornerstone of many. There are also plenty of palette-pleasing purchases to be made: homemade apple butter, candies, honey, jerky, sausage. The park map has a complete list of shops.

WILDERNESS ROAD BLACKSMITH SHOP

The blacksmith was a vital part of 1800s life, making wagon wheels, guns, horseshoes, and every kind of tool from nails to shovels. Today visitors to Silver Dollar City can see an authentic blacksmith shop and watch work done the way it was more than a hundred years ago. Metal chimes, bells, plaques, lawn ornaments, even cookware are made in the shop.

VALLEY ROAD WOODCARVERS

Whittling was a common pastime in the 1800s, and master woodcarvers continue the tradition at this unique Silver Dollar City stop. Visitors can watch woodcarvers create new works and look for finished pieces in the shop above. There is everything from fireplace mantels to small gifts and home decor.

SHOWS IN THE PARK

The music of Silver Dollar City is filled with Ozark's heritage. While the shows are always changing, the level of top-quality talent remains the same. Obviously, not every type of music will appeal to everyone, but there's enough variety here for almost every musical palette.

There are more than 40 live performances in the park every day. Some venues are small outdoor theaters. Others, like the Opera House, hold larger crowds indoors. Echo Hollow, a 4,000-seat outdoor amphitheater, hosts some of Silver Dollar City's most popular entertainment. Concerts held after the park closes provide a nice way to relax at the end of the day and avoid the rush to the parking lots. See the park map for details on the day's show offerings and times.

RESTAURANTS

They may not admit it, but plenty of people will go to a theme park for the food. Silver Dollar City is no exception. The fried food isn't going to be featured on any health channels, but folks can feel just a little better knowing it's cooked in zero–trans fat oil. No peanut oil is used. A few of the park's main restaurants are listed here; see the park map for additional concession stands, and check the park website to read the sometimes funny historical fables behind the restaurant names.

A nice souvenir is the refillable mug—purchase it once and get cheap refills on any drink in the park, even on future visits.

BREAKFAST

Restaurants on the square serve breakfast an hour before the park opens. Eva and Delilah's Bakery is an enticing stop for pastries. Molly's Mill offers a southern-style breakfast buffet.

BIG JACK'S SANDWICH SHOP

Here the customer builds the sandwich, hot or cold, choosing from a variety of meats, cheeses, breads, and toppings. Soups, salads, and desserts are also available.

LUCKY SILVER MINE RESTAURANT

In a nod to the mining profession, guests travel down a mine-shaft hallway to reach the restaurant. The menu is served buffet style and includes barbecued pork roast, beef brisket, all sorts of sides, and dessert.

MARY'S SPRINGHOUSE

Those craving Italian food will find homemade pastas, paninis, and salads at this sit-down restaurant.

MOLLY'S MILL

Located close to the park's entrance, Molly's Mill is in one of Silver Dollar City's original buildings. The restaurant is known for a down-home buffet that includes fried chicken, pot roast, catfish, macaroni and cheese, and more. Kids four and under eat free. Sometimes one of the tables is rigged to slowly rise while patrons are eating—usually not noticeable until the end of the meal, when the tabletop has become ridiculously high. That's the time to take a picture!

FAMILY RIDES

The majority of rides for the preschool set will be found in The Grand Exposition, a modern re-creation of 1800s expositions and world fairs. There is a height requirement even on these rides. Often an adult companion will suffice, but there are times when they're just going to have to grow a little.

In addition to the kiddie rides, there are a few offerings suitable for children who can handle a bit faster pace. Check the water rides section, too, for ideas on cooling off together. Remember, when planning a trip, many of these rides will not operate below 35 degrees.

FIRE IN THE HOLE

Fire in the Hole is one of the original rides at Silver Dollar City. Taking a page out of local history, the premise is that the Baldknobbers vigilantes have set the town on fire. A dark indoor roller coaster with animatronics and several small, invisible drops, this ride is tame enough for most family members. Kids can ride once they are 36 inches tall, though it may still be a bit too scary for some. It's also a nice way to find some relief from the heat without going on a water ride.

FLOODED MINE

This is a favorite family ride complete with some friendly competition. Even babies can go along on a leisurely boat ride while adults take aim with laser guns at hundreds of targets placed along the route. When targets are hit, the shooter gets points along with some kind of reaction: a mine cart may let loose, buckets may swing, lights may flash.

FRISCO SILVER DOLLAR LINE STEAM TRAIN

This relaxing 20-minute ride on an authentic steam locomotive takes passengers through the park and even into a bit of wilderness, with live narration throughout. There's a surprise "show" when bandits try to hijack the train. Don't expect academy award performances: this is just a fun skit that kids seem to really enjoy. The show portion was created in the ride's early days to entertain passengers when the train had to stop to build up enough steam to make the rest of the trip.

This ride is especially recommended at Christmastime. With holiday music playing, passengers see the light displays throughout much of the park. The show portion of the trip includes a grandfather telling the Christmas story from a rocking chair in front of his log cabin. Light displays illuminate during his narration.

ROLLER COASTERS AND OTHER THRILL RIDES

Thrill seekers will not be disappointed here. These are some of the most exciting rides around. Be aware many of these rides cannot operate if temperatures reach 40° F or below.

THE GIANT SWING

This is a swing on steroids. There are two pendulum-type swings, each with 16 people seated back to back in groups of eight. Located in the center of Wilson's Barn, the ride launches through the door at 45 mph to reach seven stories into the air. At the top, it's as though you're lying flat on your back staring into the clouds; then, just as fast, you're going backwards and facing the ground. This has to be one of the most intense thrill rides in the park. A video of the ride in action is available on the park website.

POWDERKEG

Riders embark on this experience among various barrels and imbalanced nitro-explosives fashioned after old-time powder mills. Once the nitro "explodes," riders are blasted upward onto the tracks at 53 mph in less than three seconds. There are steep hills and fast turns amid beautiful scenery of trees and a view of Table Rock Lake. Instead of a shoulder restraint, there's a lap bar that most people find comfortable and secure.

THUNDERATION

This mine-train coaster is not to be compared with the thrills of PowderKeg or Wildfire, but it still packs some pretty good exhilaration with its high speeds and spiraling helix. Cars 3 and 6 are popular because they face the opposite direction, upping the thrill factor. Many consider this one of the best mine-train coasters in the country.

WILDFIRE

It takes Wildfire just over two minutes to send riders 155 feet in the air, through three loops and a cobra roll—all at speeds of up to 66 mph. While you're screaming, be sure to enjoy the views of the Ozark Mountains. Riders are seated four to a row. Smile on this one, because somewhere along the ride your picture is going to be taken.

WATER RIDES

These rides are a fun way to cool off during the hot summer months. There are thrill rides like the American Plunge. A slower paced option suitable for all ages is found in RiverBlast. In between is the Lost River of the Ozarks.

While many people like to wear bathing suits on the water rides, Silver Dollar City requires a cover-up for anyone over the age of eight. Kids younger than eight can wear a bathing suit but they must also wear shorts. Rain ponchos can be purchased in many of the park's gift shops.

AMERICAN PLUNGE

This traditional log flume ride climbs five stories and comes crashing down the hill at 35 mph in a blast of water that will definitely leave riders soaking wet.

RIVERBLAST

This is not a fast-paced water ride, but it offers as good a chance of getting wet as any waterslide. Four riders per side are seated on benches facing outward as the boats meander very slowly outdoors. The excitement comes when spectators on the other side of the river start shooting at your boat with water guns. You can shoot back with your own super soaker, take aim at other boats, or try to hit any number of targets along the way. The ride tries to create an experience in the style of Tom Sawyer and Huck Finn. When you get off, you can take a spectator spot and blast boats with water. The soaker guns work by spinning a wheel, and by the end of the ride your arm may feel the workout.

LOST RIVER OF THE OZARKS

Up to six people can ride on this giant inner tube with seats, around bends and down several short drops. There's no doubt you'll need to dry off after this one, although there's a rumor that sitting on the far side when boarding will leave riders at least a bit dry.

Prices for shows in Branson vary greatly but, in general, plan to spend about $35-$40 for a full-price adult ticket to an evening show.

Live Shows

There are enough shows in Branson to keep people entertained for a lifetime of vacations. What surprises many is the variety of entertainment the town offers. There's certainly country/western, but there's also pop, rock and roll, gospel, and virtually every other genre of music. Beyond the concerts, there are mammoth productions like Noah the Musical, magicians and acrobats, historical theater, and more. Shows are performed morning, afternoon, and evening, and there's a show to fit just about every personality, budget, and schedule.

There are a couple of things at every Branson performance: food concessions and gift shops. Performers are almost always available to sign souvenirs during intermission and after the show.

Most shows will take the time to recognize special occasions. Mention any celebrations when making a reservation and again when arriving at the venue.

It should be noted that Branson entertainment is a little like Branson's weather. It is always changing! An all-inclusive listing is impossible as new shows are constantly being added while others may leave for a time or permanently. Also, shows change venues frequently as seating requirements or other needs change. Therefore; it is important to check theatre details for a desired show. Also, check for limited-time engagements. Performers like the Oak Ridge Boys, Johnny Mathis, Tim Conway and many more have made short appearances on the Branson stage. Finally, there are entertainers performing in Branson all year but many performances are seasonal. If visiting during the winter and early spring be sure to check for show schedules.

TICKET DEALS

Prices for shows vary but, in general, plan to spend about $35-$40 for a full-price adult ticket to an evening performance. Daytime shows generally cost less while dinner shows, of course, will be more expensive. Shows prices are designated $ = less expensive; $$ = more expensive; $$$ = most expensive. Keep in mind this designation only refers to the ticket price. A venue marked $$$ may be due to the fact the show includes a meal and is actually a good bargain.

There are a number of ways to get discounts on show tickets. Always inform the box office if you are a student or a veteran. Beyond that, many shows offer family passes good for two adults and (usually) two children, with the option of adding additional kids at a discounted rate. Always check the theatre website for the latest discount offers.

Discount ticket kiosks can be found inside practically everything with four walls. Sometimes the best place to purchase tickets is online. Several shows offer half-price deals on local websites. A good one to try is ● halfpriceozarks.com (click on "discount deals"). Besides deals on shows, there are restaurant, golf course, and other half-price offers at this site. Some certificates can be printed right away, while others must be mailed.

Keep your ticket stub when you go into a show. Often special deals are announced that will earn discounts at other shows or restaurants when presenting the stub.

A CAPELLA VOCAL AND RHYTHM GROUPS

Instruments are overrated when it comes to these performers. In fact, the only instruments they really need are their voices. Except for Jeerk. They might need a blender.

THE CAT'S PAJAMAS ✪ Must See!
(Andy Williams Moon River Theatre, 2500 W. Hwy 76
☎ 417.334.4500 🖰 vocalmeow.com) A person would be hard pressed to find more talent than what's contained in this vocal band. Using only their voices as instruments, these men leave audiences in disbelief. Beyond their impeccable musical capability, these guys have an amazing amount of energy. They don't stop except for some silly banter between numbers. Expect to hear a little of everything, including favorites from the 80s, Elvis, country, and patriotic numbers. More than anything, expect to thoroughly enjoy this show. ($)

JEERK ✪ Must See!
(Any Williams Theatre 2500 W. Hwy 76 ☎ 800.666.6094
🖰 jeerk.com) These five Swedish guys don't need to say a word to impress an audience. Neither do they need any "real" instruments. This ultimate rhythm show makes use of power tools, steel drums, hockey sticks, and more.

Dressed in t-shirts, plaid pants, and big tennis shoes, the performers might not overwhelm the fashion world—until they start moving. Underneath those tennis shoes are metal plates that transform them into modern-day tap shoes. This high-energy show is different from anything else Branson has to offer. Extraordinary lighting effects create a dramatic, urban feel. Jeerk is often on tour elsewhere so be sure to check if the show is playing in Branson during your vacation. ($)

SIX ⊗ Must See!

(Mickey Gilley Theatre, 3455 W. Hwy 76 ☎ 877.749.7469 ⊖ thesixshow.com) From the first dramatic notes, it's easy to understand why this is one of the most popular shows in Branson. It may sound like there are instruments, but it's all done with voices—even the "drums." These six real-life brothers perform a little bit of everything, from Frank Sinatra to the Beach Boys, U2, and some favorite movie sound tracks. It's a nice combination of rock and barbershop, with a touch of extremely good gospel. The brothers have a fun sense of humor and easily engage an audience. ($$)

COUNTRY

Those who love old time country will thoroughly enjoy these shows. Mickey Gilley, Buck Trent and Roy Rogers… these are just a few of the icons who paved the way for the popularity country music enjoys today. Today they appear on the Branson stage along with newcomers who continue the country legacy. For a more contemporary country sound consider Neal McCoy or Clay Cooper.

BUCK TRENT COUNTRY MUSIC SHOW

(RFD-TV The Theatre, 4080 W. Hwy 76 ☎ 417.332.2282 ⊖ claycoopertheatre.com) Anyone who enjoys classic country music is likely to love this show. Buck Trent is a country music icon from the heyday of televisions's Hee Haw series. He is unique in playing an electric banjo and is responsible for the music behind many Dolly Parton and Porter Wagoner recordings. The famous man himself is standing at the door when audience members walk into the theater to take their seats.

It's obvious from the first lively song that Trent is having the time of his life. With the bright sequined costumes and the talented performers sharing the stage, this concert pulls out all the stops. Kenny Parrott has a deep and rich country voice and sounds every bit as good as Johnny Cash singing "Ring of Fire." Likewise, Melody Hart does Dolly proud with her excellent renditions of "Jolene," "Coat of Many Colors," and more. ($)

CLAY COOPER

(Clay Cooper Theatre, 3216 W. Hwy 76 ☎ 417.332.2529 ⏾ claycoopertheatre.com) Clay Cooper has been singing classic
and contemporary country music in Branson since the age of 16. Now in his own large and comfortable venue, he presents an action-packed variety show. Clay shares the stage with cowboy Johnny Onestar of America's Got Talent, who shows off his work with the lasso. Part rhythm and part comedy, the Buckets N Boards duo offers talented silliness, and comedian Matt Gumm brings more laughs. The Country Express Cloggers entertain with precision footwork. Clay's young son, Colton, performs in several numbers, and Clay performs plenty of country music himself. During the holiday season Clay transforms the second half of the show. $$

DALENA DITTO

(Hamner Barber Theatre 3090 Shepherd of the Hills Expy ☎ 888.335.2080 ⏾ hamnerbarber.com) It's not uncommon
for this warmhearted and personable talent to pick a dance

Live Shows

partner from the audience. Ditto is the daughter of Tennessee Floyd and performs classic country music, from Patsy Cline to Marty Robbins. The Iowa soprano is backed by a six-piece band known as The Boys. Impressionist Jeff Brandt also joins the show performing comedy and music. During the holiday season enjoy seasonal favorites. ($)

MICKEY GILLEY

(Mickey Gilley Theatre, 3455 W. Hwy 76 ☎ 800.334.1936 🖰 gilleys.com) Watching this legend of country music perform is not only fun but also inspiring, since his remarkable recovery from a serious fall in 2009. Mickey Gilley is one of the best-loved entertainers in Branson.

The mechanical bull parked in the center of the theater lobby will take people back to Gilley's in Texas and the movie Urban Cowboy. Gilley's show includes his many number-one songs, and throughout the performance Gilley tells stories about his career and growing up in Louisiana with cousins Jerry Lee Lewis and Jimmy Swaggart. He's supported by two excellent backup singers and a live band; some of its members have performed with him for decades. Band member and comedian Joey Riley is a funny addition to the performance. He and Gilley ad-lib much of the routine, and it's not unusual to see them both fall apart laughing. ($)

NEAL MCCOY ✪ Must See!

(Clay Cooper Theatre 3216 W Hwy 76 ☎ 417.332.2529 🖰 claycoopertheatre.com) Neal McCoy is, in every way, a contemporary country music star, from his black cowboy hat and tight Wranglers to his one-of-a-kind stage presence.

Country music legend Mickey Gilley says McCoy is one of the greatest entertainers he's ever seen. He's been named TNN/Music City News "Entertainer of the Year" two times.

It's impossible to describe McCoy's show, because it's different every night. He sings whatever comes to him or whatever the audience wants to hear. The band never misses a beat and has an easy rapport with the star. McCoy also has a random sense of humor and split-second wit. No one knows what will come out of his mouth next, but there's a pretty good chance it's going to make the audience laugh. ($$$)

ROY ROGERS AND THE HIGH RIDERS
(RFD-TV The Theatre, 4080 W. Hwy 76 ☎ 417.332.2282 ☗ royrogers.com) Walking into this show is like walking onto the set of an old western. Cactus plants are scattered about the stage along with a horse buggy and other cowboy staples, against the backdrop of a mountain scene. Taking the stage is Roy Rogers Junior ("Dusty"), son of cowboy legend Roy Rogers. Dusty's own son, Dustin, also performs. The harmonic High Riders accompany the famous family members. There are no special effects or fancy dancers here, just simple cowboy songs, stories about growing up with Roy Rogers and Dale Evans, and clips of Roy and other legendary screen cowboys. Ask about discounts for veterans and active military when ordering tickets.

Diehard Roy Rogers fans might be interested to know about two themed accommodations that are part of the Westgate Branson Woods. Guests may request the Roy Rogers Bunkhouse or the Dale Evans Ranch House. ($)

COMEDY

Comedy is part of almost every performance in Branson but these shows are dedicated to making audiences laugh.

3 REDNECK TENORS

(Americana Theatre, 2905 W. Hwy 76 ☎ 417.339.4663 📱 3rednecktenors.com) Many are familiar with this group from the popular show, "America's Got Talent." If that doesn't ring a bell, picture three overweight guys sporting mullets and white "Saturday Night Fever" style suits singing Bee Gees music -- in perfect operatic pitch. It may look bad but it sounds great.

The show is a tongue-in-cheek story of some redneck buddies (Billy Bob, Billy Joe and Billy Billie) being discovered in a Paris, Texas trailer park. Audiences follow them on a hilarious journey to Carnegie Hall. Be prepared to see these rather hairy-chested men don evening gowns along the way.

It's unlikely one could find a wider range of music in any show. Audiences will hear everything from the Love Boat theme song to Hound Dog (opera style, of course) and You Light Up My Life.

The show is funny enough to keep kids and adults entertained. During the second half of the show the mullets are gone and there is an opportunity to hear the tenors' real-life journey as well as some true opera performances.

COMEDY JAMBOREE

(Grand Country Square 1945 W. Hwy 76 ☎ 417.335.2484 📱 grandcountry.com) This is a vaudeville-style comedy starring Apple Jack and Guppy, who dress as different zany characters throughout the show. In addition to the jokes, there is seriously good music by country vocalist Todd Bradshaw, accompanied by a talented group of musicians and dancers. ($)

JIM STAFFORD'S ROCK 'N' ROLL COMEDY JAM

(3440 W. Hwy 76 ☎ 417.335.8080 🖱 jimstafford.com) One of the unique things about Jim Stafford's show is the way he can make audience members feel at home. Being in his theater feels like sitting in the entertainer's living room and listening as he tells a few good jokes. The humor is clean enough for the kids to hear and funny enough to make the adults laugh out loud.

Opening the show is RockIT, a talented live band performing classic rock music. Jim's gifted teenage children, Sheaffer and G.G., perform in various numbers. Sheaffer's ability on the piano is as impressive as his father's guitar pickin'. In addition to the classic rock numbers, Stafford fans will hear him perform his hits "Spiders and Snakes," "My Girl Bill," and "Cow Patti." One of the humorous highlights is when Jim starts throwing cow patties (fake, of course) into the audience. Even parents with the youngest visitors are made to feel welcome with a "cry room" in the back where they can take fussy ones and still watch the show.

Along with comedy and music, this show incorporates an impressive laser light show as well as a 3-D experience. This is an affordable venue for larger broods thanks to an available family pass. The price covers two adult tickets and all children under seventeen. ($$)

Live Shows

PAUL HARRIS AND THE CLEVERLY'S

(White House Theatre, 775 Gretna Rd ☎ 417.335.2396
🖱 paulharriscomedy.com) Paul Harris and his band have made a name for themselves opening for country greats Blake Shelton, Jeff Foxworthy, Little Big Town and others. The group's alter-ego, The Cleverly's, found a sensational following on YouTube. The Cleverly's make regular appearances in the show.

Harris continues to gain popularity in Branson with hilarious jokes and some of the best bluegrass music to be found. Even those who aren't fans of bluegrass will easily appreciate the outstanding talent. Those who come for the comedy will not be disappointed. The stories Harris shares are outrageous and downright hilarious.

In the second half of the show The Cleverly trio (made up of five men) make an appearance wearing the worst of suits paired with even worse cowboy hats. They make Jeff Foxworthy look sophisticated. Introductions include a commercial fisherman who "caught the crabs." While they're not the classiest bunch they can definitely keep an audience entertained with unbeatable bluegrass and backwoods comedy.

There is some adult humor in this show although nothing with offensive language. Children seem to enjoy the comedy and jokes not meant for their age level are told in a way that is, thankfully, over their heads.

Guests looking for some country fare can enjoy a chicken-fried-steak dinner with the show.

YAKOV SMIRNOFF

(470 Hwy 248 ☎ 866.328.3733 🖱 yakov.com) In a town where getting around requires color-coded maps, Yakov Smirnoff gives tourists a little help. No one could miss the enormous billboard practically shouting at cars driving by on the highway. After exiting, all one has to do is look for Yakov's giant head. The oversized bust sits right in front of the entrance to his theater.

While the Russian immigrant is billed as a comedian, he's serious about laughter and passionate about his mission "to experience happiness and teach it through comedy and sensitivity." In the midst of comical stories about immigrating to America and the cultural predicaments it raised, Yakov weaves a serious message about loving this country and one another. Yakov also spends time on philosophical reflections about love and laughter as they relate to marital relationships. Yakov is known for the phrase, "What a country!" After experiencing the laughter and tears in this rollercoaster ride of a show, people may well say, "What an American!" ($$)

ACROBATS

These visually stunning shows make audiences gasp at the daring feats of the performers. The acts are simultaneously graceful and powerful and have proven to be popular among Branson audiences.

ACROBATS OF CHINA/NEW SHANGHAI CIRCUS

(New Shanghai Theatre, 645 State Hwy 165 ☎ 417.336.8888 🖱 acrobatsofchina.com) Many compare this show to Cirque du

Soleil. It is filled with "do not try this at home" contortion acts. Each segment opens with narration about an aspect of Chinese culture. Demonstrations include fast-moving performances like the "hoop divers" along with acts that require some audience patience as performers set up intricate acrobatic maneuvers. The awe-inspiring acts are worth the wait. The background music is Chinese, and some American audiences may find two hours of this to be a little monotonous. The Acrobats of China is a fine choice for those looking for something different from Branson's country music fare. ($$)

CULTURAL/HISTORICAL

One can enjoy extraordinary entertainment from around the world in Branson. Experience the culture of the Biblical era, the talent of Ireland and China, or witness the story that made Branson become one of the most popular tourist destinations in the country. The Shepherd of the Hills Outdoor Drama has been proudly performed by locals for over five decades.

LEGENDS OF KUNG FU ✪ Must See!
**(White House Theatre, 775 Gretna Rd. ☎ 417.335.2396
🖱 kungfubranson.com)** This is not simply a kung fu fighting show. Rather, it tells the story of a young boy beginning with the day he is left by his mother to be trained in a Chinese temple. It shows his journey of making mistakes and conquering fear and pride and ultimately becoming a master of Kung Fu.

There is reference to Buddhist beliefs. The sets are beautiful and the action is exciting. An enormous cast includes lots of children with great acrobatic talent. One little boy does multiple backflips, landing on his head. Be aware that short narration pieces are lip-synced by actors because of language barriers. There are also reference to Buddhist beliefs. Legends of Kung Fu is a dramatic, graceful, and powerful presentation.

Guests also have the option of enjoying a Chinese meal with the show. ($$)

NOAH THE MUSICAL ✪ Must See!

(Sight and Sound Theatre, 1001 Shepherd of the Hills Expy ☎ 800.377.1277 ▯ sight-sound.com) True to its name, this theater provides visitors with magnificent lighting and sound effects. Mammoth sets and both live and animatronic animals re-create the Biblical era of Noah. During the second half of the show, audience members will feel as though they've been transported into the very heart of Noah's ark for his 40-day-and-night journey. First-class voices entertain while telling the story; some dramatic liberty is taken in interpreting what life was like during the era. For restless little ones there is a cry room at the top of the balcony. It is basic but does have a window allowing parents see the show.

An hour-long behind-the-scenes tour offers the opportunity to see the animals up close. Visitors explore the stage and dressing rooms, meet some of the actors, and learn some of the secrets that go into putting on the production.

This theater rotates the stories of Noah, Joseph, and the Miracle of Christmas. All are presented with the same quality of sets and storytelling. ($$$)

SHEPHERD OF THE HILLS OUTDOOR DRAMA ⭐ Must See!

(5586 W. Hwy 76 ☎ 417.334.4191 📍 oldmatt.com) Anyone who wants to understand the history of the Ozarks and how this place became so popular should see this show. It has been running for more than 50 years and has given more performances than any other outdoor historical drama in the nation. The enactment of Harold Bell Wright's story, *The Shepherd of the Hills*, takes place in an outdoor amphitheater that actually sits on the homestead site of John and Anna Ross, with whom Wright stayed on his first visits to this area.

With a few exceptions, the acting won't win many awards; these are local people telling their local history. Some have been part of the play since it began in 1960. As in the novel, there is plenty of drama, with gunfights, brawls, fire, love, and murder. There are more than 80 actors, 40 horses and other animals, and a 1908 DeWitt vehicle. All of this comes together to portray a story of the Ozarks that is part fiction and part reality. The entire audience is invited to participate in a square dance within the story. ($$)

TWELVE IRISH TENORS

(Branson Variety Theater, 2701 W. Hwy 76 ☎ 417.334.2500 📍 bransonvarietytheater.com) This show is exactly what it says: 12 Irish tenors. But the name could be a little more descriptive. It could say 12 of the most talented (and great looking) Irish tenors around. Together they perform songs made famous by Barry Manilow, Celine Dion, Josh Groban, Frank Sinatra, and the Beatles, along with Irish opera and traditional Irish songs such as "Danny Boy." There is also plenty of silly banter between the tenors, and some fun audience interaction. This show is well worth the time and is a great value. ($)

DINNER SHOWS

These shows offer a good value considering the included dinner. Some offer the meal as an option while, for others, it is a part of the actual experience. Check with the theatre to see if special dietary needs can be accommodated. Be sure to have cash to tip the hard-working dinner servers.

CIRCLE B SUPPER SHOW

(200 Jess-Jo Pkwy ☎ 417.336.3540 🖱 circlebshow.com) This may be one of the most informal and friendly places in town. The Horn family welcomes guests with yee-haw enthusiasm, baskets of free popcorn, and episodes of the old Lone Ranger and Roy Rogers television shows. Kids can be informally deputized to help fight the "cornbread bandit," a silly start to the show. The show itself is performed by the Riders of the Circle B, and it's designed to pay musical homage to the American cowboy. The songs aren't country, they're cowboy—numbers like "Don't Fence Me In," "Desperado," and "Red River Valley." While the comedy portion is a little painful, the music is good, and there's plenty of fun to be had at the Circle B.

The food is definitively cowboy: chicken, sausage, beans, fries, applesauce, cornbread, and dessert. If one plate isn't enough, the Horns will keep serving the sides until everyone's full. Kids' meals are also available. This is an affordable venue. Ticket prices are about the price of other shows that do not serve a meal. A family pass is also available and includes two adults and up to three children. For those not wanting dinner the show is even less expensive. ($)

DIXIE STAMPEDE ★ Must See!

(1525 W Hwy 76 ☎ 800.520.5544 🖲 dixiestampede.com) If you could only see one show in Branson, Dolly Parton's Dixie Stampede should be among your top choices, especially if there are various ages in your group. Kids can let loose any pent-up energy by kicking and stomping during comical contests between North and South.

The action takes place in an enormous horse arena where Dolly herself welcomes guests from a large video screen. Dinner is a hearty four-course meal served during the performance, which includes stunt riders, comedy, and patriotic music. One thing missing from the table: silverware. Food at the Dixie Stampede is all about fingers so enjoy getting dirty and rest assured there will be a hot towel delivered to clean up.

An hour before the arena opens, there's a preshow in the Carriage Room. If celebrating a special occasion, let the ticket agent or an usher know and it will be announced during the preshow.

Those suffering from allergies or asthma should take precautions. While it's exceptionally clean, this is a dirt arena with live animals. If you want to be close to the animals, consider attending the final show of the day. At the end of that performance, riders line up around the arena and guests can take pictures and even pet the horses.

At Christmas, the entire arena is transformed with lights and decorations, spectacular costumes, and holiday music. The games are still a part of the fun, but North and South transform into Red and Green. There's a dramatic live Nativity scene complete with angels flying overhead. ($$$)

Live Shows

IT

(3425 W. Hwy 76 ☎ 417.334.0076 🖱 hughes-brothers.com) The Hughes Brothers offer a nice dinner option before their show. Meals include a choice of pork tenderloin, chicken breast with red potatoes, vegetable medley, salad, rolls, dessert, and beverage. It's not uncommon for the personable brothers to visit with dinner guests. ($$)

LEGENDS OF KUNG FU ✪ Must See!

(White House Theatre, 775 Gretna Rd. ☎ 417.335.2396 🖱 kungfubranson.com) Guests attending the Legends of Kung Fu show have the option of enjoying a cultural meal with the show. The menu includes an Asian salad and spring roll followed by Springfield cashew chicken over rice and glazed bacon-wrapped green beans.

PAUL HARRIS AND THE CLEVERLY'S

(White House Theatre, 775 Gretna Rd ☎ 417.335.2396 🖱 paulharriscomedy.com) Get your fill of southern cooking before seeing the hilarious Paul Harris and the Cleverly's. Battered country fried steak is served alongside mashed potatoes and gravy. Veggies include salad and green beans. Top it off with caramel apple pie. A vegetarian option offers a grilled portabello mushroom in place of the steak.

SHOWBOAT BRANSON BELLE ✪ Must See!

(4800 Hwy 165 ☎ 800.475.9370 🖱 showboatbransonbelle.com) For visitors unable to decide whether to hit the lake or the Strip, the Showboat Branson Belle is a perfect combination. Board the 700-passenger paddlewheeler at White River Landing for a two-hour cruise of

Table Rock Lake that includes a three-course lunch or dinner along with some of the area's top dancers, musicians, and comedy acts. Headlining the entertainment are fiddling aerialist Janice Martin and the male vocal group The Showmen, who perform music from the 60s onward with an impressive vocal range.

Food is cooked onboard. For an extra fee, guests can order off the menu and dine in the private Paddle Wheel Club with views of the water. (It's worth the extra cost.) Tables are for groups of four, so parties of two may be seated with other guests. Captain's Row guests may also order off the menu but are seated in a section of the general dining room. Between dinner and the show, guests can roam the ship to enjoy the lake views and visit the captain's wheelhouse.

The size of the showboat and the relatively calm conditions on Table Rock Lake make for a very smooth ride. The cruise is free for those celebrating birthdays or, if it isn't operating on their birthdays, their half-birthdays! $$$

SONS OF THE PIONEERS CHUCKWAGON DINNER SHOW

(5586 W. Hwy 76 ☎ 417.334.4191 ▮ oldmatt.com) This is more than a Branson show: it is a piece of American history. The Sons of the Pioneers, with their distinctive cowboy sound, began in 1934. In fact, Roy Rogers was one of the original members of the group. While listening to music sung by cowboys and about cowboys, guests partake of an outdoor western meal (filling though definitely not fine dining). These are award-winning fiddlers, banjo players, and vocalists displaying impeccable harmony. $

YAKOV'S DINNER ADVENTURE

(470 Hwy 248 ☎ 417.823.8645 🖱 yakov.com) This is entirely different from Yakov's comedy show. In fact, while he narrates this story via video recording, Yakov does not make an actual appearance.

The show is about the love between a clown and a dancer in a Russian circus. Before the pair eventually escapes to the land of the free, there are dramatic circus acts from a revolving lineup that may include Andrei the clown, a human slinky, a unicyclist, trained dogs and cats, and lots of dancers. There are dancing poodles, a dancing fire-eater, and mesmerizing Russian dancers. Even the audience gets to be part of this show during some stunts. The meal is served during intermission. Kids' meals called "Yak in the Box" are available. This is a reasonably priced venue with tickets priced below what most shows cost without a meal. Elite seating costs a little more. Family passes including up to five tickets are available. ($)

HOLIDAY SHOWS

Branson is, without a doubt, a holiday destination. Like the town itself, many of the shows undergo a complete holiday transformation. These special venues have the same quality and magic for which Branson performances are known.

CHRISTMAS ON THE TRAIL

(5586 W. Hwy 76 ☎ 800.653.6288 🖱 christmasonthetrail.com) This is a cowboy celebration of Christmas, with country singing and cowboy grub, in the pavilion at the Shepherd of the Hills. The entertainers seat themselves on bales of hay in front of a starry backdrop. A comedic emcee adds some silly camaraderie. Santa makes an appearance, handing out candy canes to young dinner guests. The music includes trail songs and Christmas favorites. The audience is invited to sing along during several numbers. The meal includes chicken, potatoes, three-bean chili, cornbread, corn on the cob, and Dutch oven apple cobbler made over the campfire.

Included with a ticket to this show is admission to the Shepherd of the Hills Inspiration Tower and the drive-through Trail of Lights, along with a complimentary cup of coffee, hot chocolate, or spiced cider. ($$$)

MIRACLE OF CHRISTMAS
(1001 Shepherd of the Hills Expy ☎ 800.377.1277

🖱 sight-sound.com) A large theater and cast, realistic costumes, real animals, flying angels, spectacular set designs, and powerful musical scores make the first Christmas come alive. The stage covers the front and sides of the auditorium, enveloping the audience in the drama. The show begins with a look at what was going on politically under the rule of the Romans and in the lives of some of the Jewish people at the time of Jesus' birth. Events are interpreted, and characters are created in order to tell the Biblical story. ($$$)

HOLLYWOOD'S CHRISTMAS SPECTACULAR
(Branson Variety Theatre 2701 W. Hwy 76 ☎ 417.336.2500

🖱 bransonvarietytheater.com) If you love movies and Christmas, buy a ticket to see Hollywood's Christmas Spectacular. The show is a two-hour journey through some of the big screen's greatest holiday moments. Audiences watch scenes like the 1977 Christmas special with Bing Crosby and David Bowie singing "Little Drummer Boy," while reliving the music through live song and dance numbers. Other movie clips displayed on stage include *White Christmas*, *Home Alone*, *Mary Poppins*, *Love Actually*, *Sister Act* and even *The Grinch*.

The performance manages to be both fun and sentimental. A stirring tribute to servicemen coming home to their families is especially poignant. The routines are fast-paced with plenty of dancing, including an impressive tap number. This show, like just about every one in Branson, changes from year to year so it's possible there may be different movies or songs performed. Still, you can count on beautiful sets and costumes along with plenty of musical talent. ($$)

INSTRUMENTAL

Parents will probably feel the need to sign their kids up for violin lessons after watching these performances where instruments take center stage. These performers have impressive talent and plenty of personality.

DUTTONS

(Dutton Family Theater, 3454 W. Hwy 76 ☎ 417.332.2772 ☗ theduttons.com) Many will recognize this family as 2007 finalists on America's Got Talent. They've gone on to open their own theater, hotel, and restaurant in the heart of Branson. Members of the family continue to receive awards, like "Branson's best instrumentalist," female entertainer of the year, and best band in Branson

Most people will remember the way the siblings play the violin, banjo, and just about any other stringed instrument put in their hands, but they also sing and dance with the same level of talent. Parents Dean and Sheila, their six grown children, and nearly 20 grandkids all take part in this high-energy show. Guests love seeing the family during intermission running concessions, selling fudge in the lobby, and, of course, signing autographs. This is a fantastic show for all ages. ($$)

SHOJI TABUCHI

(3260 Shepherd of the Hills Expy ☎ 417.334.7469
⬤ shoji.com) Branson may be the only place one could find a Japanese American violinist with a passion for country music. Entertaining here for more than two decades, Shoji is a popular choice among tourists. He loves country but also incorporates swing, polka, gospel, rock, and even rap. The show has a glitzy feel, especially during Broadway segments with other musicians and dancers. Shoji's daughter, Christina, is a big part of the show. A new element is a nod to Shoji's Japanese heritage with an impressive taiko drum performance. There are 25 drums of various sizes and styles played amid beautiful costumes and sets.

The fanciest part of the Shoji experience doesn't take place inside the auditorium. The restroom facilities have received numerous accolades, including the title of "nation's best restroom"! Highlights include a billiard table in the men's room. A Parisian marble fireplace and fresh flowers set the ladies room apart. ($$$)

MUSICAL ERA SHOWS

These are shows dedicated to particular eras of music. Some focus on the 50s and 60s, while others take audiences on a trip through many generations of sound.

RANKIN BROTHERS CLASSIC MUSIC REVUE ✪ Must See!
(Mickey Gilley Theater, 3455 W. Hwy 76 ☎ 800.334.1936
🖱 **rankinbrothers.com)** The Rankin Brothers are fairly new on the Branson scene, but they've already earned something of a cult following. On a recent visit, this author sat next to a woman celebrating her 250th time seeing the Rankins. The woman on the other side proudly showed off her "I've Been Rankinized" button.

It doesn't take long to see what makes these brothers so popular. They're good looking, have appealing personalities, and demonstrate astonishing talent. When Mark opens his mouth, it's nothing less than shocking to hear that kind of range and that mature and rich a sound. He does Neil Diamond, Elvis, Bob Dylan, and even Sonny Bono effortlessly. In fact, the costume he wears as Elvis was made to specifications for one of Elvis' actual costumes. Matt finds his niche with a Buddy Holly tribute that even impresses the late singer's wife.

Together Mark and Matt Rankin perform a long medley of 50s and 60s music. They are backed by the capable Rankinettes, who also perform several numbers on their own. This is definitely a show worth seeing. ($$)

RED, HOT AND BLUE ⊗ Must See!

(Red, Hot and Blue, Clay Cooper, 3216 W. Hwy 76
☎ **417.332.2529 ⛊ claycoopertheatre.com)** Some call this the
hardest-working cast in Branson, with a dozen singers and
dancers putting themselves through 100 costume changes and
performing 50 songs. The music takes audiences back to the
ragtime jazz era and on through the big band sound, the music
of the 50s and 60s, and the disco decade of the 70s. This is a
fast-paced and exciting show to watch. The costuming is some
of the best in Branson. Every member of Red Hot and Blue is
highly talented; tenor Jeremy Rabe may be the comedian of the
bunch, but his voice is remarkable.

During the holiday season, expect Christmas music to be
mixed in, from an inspiring "Carol of the Bells" to a powerful
"O Holy Night" solo. ($)

SHAKE RATTLE AND ROLL

(Branson Variety Theater, 2701 W Hwy 76 ☎ 417.334.2500
⛊ **bransonvarietytheatre.com)** This high energy show takes audiences back to another time. Members of the live band wear
white suits and swing their instruments to the beat of "Rock
around the Clock" and other 50's favorites. There's no shortage
of poodle skirts or pony tails in this large cast of singers and
dancers. Enjoy songs like That'll Be the Day, Peggy Sue, Good
Golly Miss Molly, Great Balls of Fire, Blueberry Hill and
many more. The talented cast hit the mark in this nostalgic
performance.

FAMILY/KIDS

Just about every show in Branson is suitable for kids, but the following are produced expressly for them. Fortunately, the talent and entertainment values are good enough to keep the adults from squirming.

AMAZING PETS

(Grand Country Square, 1945 W. Hwy 76 ☎ 888.506.6278 🖱 grandcountry.com/s_amazing_pets.asp) This is a touring show held at the Grand Country Theatre when it is in town. The stars are mainly trained house pets wearing ridiculously cute costumes and performing stunts that make audiences laugh and cheer. Family passes are available and include two adults and up to six children. ($$)

ROCK U MENTALLY ⊗ Must See!

(Dick Clark's American Bandstand Theatre, 1600 W Highway 76 ☎ 417.339.3003 🖱 rockumentally.com) Stimulate your imagination, Rock U Mentalize your education! That's the motto of this high-energy show for kids. The songs are written by the show's creator, Bucky Heard. He and his wife, AJ, are staples in Branson and star in some of the town's most popular shows. This show's message is closest to their hearts.

Delving into real-life issues kids face, Rock U Mentally uses humor, dance, contemporary music, games, and loveable characters to send messages about bullying, dealing with strangers, taking care of the planet, responsibility, and using your imagination. There's plenty of opportunity for audience participation, in games like "peanut butter ping pong" and "embarrass the parent." This is a show people of all ages can enjoy together. It is seasonal, so call or go online for a show schedule. ($)

TODD OLIVER AND FRIENDS

(The Americana Theatre, 2905 W. Hwy 76 ☎ 417.339.4663
☮ funnydog.com) A featured entertainer on the Showboat Branson Belle for 13 years, Todd Oliver has proven so popular that he has launched his own show at the Americana Theater together with his three talking dogs, Irving, Lucy, and Elvis. Oliver's a ventriloquist, but these dogs are no dummies. They're real animals and, together with Todd, make some really funny comedy. New to Todd's quirky family are wooden characters Pops, Miss Lilly, and Joey, along with Oliver's Smiling Eyes Band.

This is truly a show that will make kids and adults laugh out loud. Audience members especially enjoy the opportunity to meet these lovable dogs; get some pictures and even scratch their ears after the show. ($$)

WALTZING WATERS

(3617 W. Hwy 76 ☎ 417.334.4144
☮ bransonwaltzingwaters.com) Waltzing Waters is one of Branson's most economical entertainment choices. The show is entertaining and beautiful and runs every hour from 10 a.m. to 10 p.m. seven days a week. Even babies are mesmerized by the 40,000 gallons of water that seems to perform in conjunction with the music being played. Colors add to the dramatic feel of the 40-minute show. Afterwards you can go behind the scenes to see how it all works. A family pass which includes two adults and two children is available. ($)

POP/CLASSICAL

These music shows will appeal to many types of musical tastes. There is a wide variety of songs and style in the shows, from classical to chart-topping pop hits.

CASSANDRE', THE VOICE OF AN ANGEL

(The Americana Theatre, 2905 W. Hwy 76 ☎ 417.339.4663 ▌thevoiceofanangel.com) A stunning soprano backed by a live orchestra, Cassandre' Faimon-Haygood delivers lovely renditions of popular songs from the 40s to the 70s. She has an effortless rapport with the audience and appears to be enjoying every moment onstage. During her many costume changes, the band takes center stage. Tenor Jeremy Rabe makes occasional special appearances to sing with Cassandre'.

Cassandre' is from Nebraska, but alter ego Aunt Irma brings a completely different persona. With a big wig, big house dress, big "assets," and big accent, Aunt Irma adds comedy to the show. During the Christmas season, the second half of the show is dedicated to holiday songs and costumes. ($)

GEORGE DYER ⊗ Must See!

(Dutton Theater, 3454 W. Hwy 76 ☎ 888.388.8661 ▌georgedyer.com) Fans of Josh Groban or Michael Buble will appreciate this performance. George Dyer's voice is every bit as melodic, and his show is unique in Branson. Dyer performs a number of Broadway musical numbers, including a riveting "The Phantom of the Opera," along with endearing love songs and his own version of Groban's "If You Just Believe." Dyer has a big sense of humor and a way of making sure the audience has a good time. His family is part of the act, his son playing sax and his daughter singing. Everything is performed with a live band.

During the Christmas season, Dyer sings favorite holiday songs during the second half of the show. His interpretation of "O Holy Night" may alone be worth the price of a ticket. ($)

TRIBUTE SHOWS

Some entertainers make such an impact with their music that the industry is changed forever. These performances pay tribute to some of these legendary talents.

EAGLES TAKE IT TO THE LIMIT ⊗ Must See!
(God and Country Theater, 1840 W Hwy 76 ☎ 417.334.6806
⬯ eaglesbranson.com) Eagles fans should close their eyes and let their ears believe they are listening to Don Henley and the rest of the band. It won't be hard to do. These musicians know the songs and the intricate harmony of the Eagles. There are no dancers or comedians in this production. The show is simply an impressive tribute concert filled with favorite Eagles songs, like "Love Will Keep Us Alive," "Take It Easy," "Hotel California," and "Take it to the Limit." The only complaint is that there's no dance floor. ($)

THE ELVIS EXPERIENCE
(Caravelle Theatre, 3446 W Hwy 76 ☎ 417.336.6100
⬯ tonyroielvisexperience.com) Elvis might be dead, but his voice is alive and well in the person of Tony Roi. In this show, the award-winning impersonator performs favorites and lesser-known numbers. His voice is absolutely Elvis, even when he's

talking. He has the hair and the costumes to match the sound, too, though he's thinner than Elvis. Roi performs with a live band and two female backup singers. He's quite interactive with the audience and obviously enjoys bringing back memories for many of those attending his show. ($)

HANK WILLIAMS REVISITED

(3562 Shepherd of the Hills Expy ☎ 800.419.4832 📱 bransonimax.com) Anyone who enjoys Hank Williams music will want to make a point of seeing this show. Tim Hadler effortlessly performs the songs of the legendary country singer and songwriter, and throughout the show he tells stories from Williams' life. Hadler's appreciation for Williams is evident, and audience members can't help but share it after watching this performance. ($)

LEGENDS IN CONCERT

(Dick Clark's American Bandstand Theatre, 1600 W. Hwy 76 ☎ 417.339.3003 📱 legendsinconcert.com) This is a high-energy show by impersonators performing as some of America's most famous talents. Elvis and the Blues Brothers are staples throughout the year. Other acts may include Alan Jackson, Britney Spears, Whitney Houston, Michael Jackson, and Little Richard. Screens on either side of the stage show video clips of the real artists while their impersonators re-enact their performances dressed in replica costumes.

In the upstairs portion of the theater, dinner is available before or during the show. Food is served from Dick Clark's American Bandstand Grill. ($$)

LEROY NEW PERFORMS MARTY ROBBINS

(3562 Shepherd of the Hills Expy ☎ 800.419.4832
☝ **bransonimax.com)** Leroy New tells the story of Marty
Robbins through music. The small venue gives audience
members the opportunity to build a friendly rapport with this
versatile entertainer, who performs hits like "El Paso," "Devil
Woman," and "Falina." The band is impressive. ($)

LIVERPOOL LEGENDS

(The Mansion Theater, 189 Expressway Ln ☎ 417.239.1333
☝ **themansiontheater.com)** Beatles fans will not be disappointed
with this show. Hand-picked by George Harrison's sister,
Louise, these four musicians transport audience members
to another time without using any added soundtracks. They
look and sound like the Beatles, all the way down to individual
mannerisms. They even play vintage instruments. Songs span
the life of the band from its beginnings through its members'
solo careers. There are video clips from actual Beatles performances. Often Louise Harrison makes an appearance to share
memories and answer audience questions about her famous
brother and the iconic band. The Liverpool Legends members
are more than approachable after the concert, signing autographs and meeting fans. Dancing is welcome during this show.
Be aware that there are special lighting effects, and it can get a
little loud. ($$)

VARIETY

These shows have a little bit of everything: comedy, music,
dance and more.

ANDY WILLIAMS

(2500 W Hwy 76 ☎ 417.334.4500 🖱 andywilliams.com) The famous tenor is still going strong after decades of entertaining. His beautiful Moon River Theater stands out among the rest on the Strip. The production is patterned after his popular television variety show of the 60s and 70s. Andy sings favorites like "I Need You Baby" and, naturally, "Moon River," accompanied by young singers and dancers. Sharing the stage are the star's latest hand-picked acts, including the world's fastest fiddle players, Russian dancers, and a believable Elvis impersonator. Those familiar with the original variety show will enjoy an appearance by "Cookie Bear."

Andy only performs during the fall and Christmas seasons. His is the voice behind many classic versions of holiday songs. ($$)

BALDKNOBBERS JAMBOREE

(2835 W Hwy 76 ☎ 417.334.4528 🖱 baldknobbers.com) The Baldknobbers and Branson are virtually synonymous. This was the town's first show, opening on Branson's lakefront in 1959. Back in the day, the Mabe brothers hoped to sell a dozen tickets in order to put on a lakefront show for local fishermen. Today the Mabe family plays in a 1,500-seat auditorium on Branson's now-famous Strip. The Mabes are the Baldknobbers, and the second and third generations carry on the tradition of comedy and music for which the family has become famous.

This show is all about variety. There are 19 people on stage either singing, dancing, playing instruments, or acting ridiculous. The musicians perform old-time and contemporary country, religious, and patriotic numbers. The comedy is hillbilly humor. That means guys with bad teeth (or no teeth) dressed in overalls and baseball caps and acting clueless. The twist is how the hillbillies "put one over" on the straight man. Stub Meadows, Hargus Marcel, and Droopy Drawers are favorite characters for many Branson visitors.

The Baldknobbers put on a completely new show every year. During the holidays the show's second half is filled with Christmas music. A family pass is available throughout the year. ($)

BRETT FAMILY

(Dick Clark's American Bandstand Theater, 1600 W. Hwy 76 ☎ 417.336.4222 🖱 brettfamily.com) Mom and Dad Brett and their three grown children sing and dance to music from various decades and genres. Their strong religious faith is evident in gospel numbers. A moving patriotic tribute is one of the show's highlights. Each member has a powerful voice, and together they make a powerful group harmony. A special Christmas show offers seasonal classics, hymns, and other holiday-themed music. ($)

HAMNER BARBER VARIETY SHOW ⊗ Must See!

(3090 Shepherd of the Hills Expy ☎ 417.334.4363 🖱 hamnerbarber.com) This show has everything Branson audiences crave. Dave and Denise Hamner provide the suspense with their thrilling illusions. Exotic birds appear out of thin air and soar overhead in a beautiful and graceful act. Jim Barber, on the other hand, wouldn't necessarily be described as beautiful. In fact, "dummy" would be a better term. That's exactly what he is in a hilarious role reversal: Seville, his wooden partner, "carries" Barber onto the stage as the dummy. It only gets stranger (and funnier) from there. Barber's award-winning ventriloquism leaves people laughing and scratching their heads at the same time.

In a town full of patriotic tributes, this show provides one of the most moving. Hamner and Barber spent two years developing the show's finale, "Thank You's Not Enough." This in itself may be worth the price of a ticket. Stunning sets, music, dancing, and high-quality talent makes this one of Branson's "must-see" shows.

During the holiday season, Hamner Barber presents "Wings of Christmas." The second half of this show features Christmas magic, songs, and a magnificent appearance by the feathered cast. Family passes and group rates are available at all of the Hamner Barber performances. ($)

HAYGOODS ⭐ Must See!
(RFD-TV The Theatre, 4080 W Hwy 76 ☎ 417.332.2282
🖱 **thehaygoods.com)** "Wow." That's likely to be the first thought when watching the Haygoods. "Wow" because they are real-life siblings. "Wow" because the seven brothers and one sister can all sing, dance, and play instruments, and they do it all really, really well. "Wow" because the harmony is as good as that of any top vocal group.

The Haygoods started as kids, playing for nearly a decade at Silver Dollar City until they moved into their own theater. They do a wide variety of music, including 50s, Motown, Beatles, gospel, and plenty of country. The Haygoods, unlike most other shows, completely reinvent their performance every year. During the holiday season the group does a Christmas performance during the show's second half.

It's not unusual to be part of a standing ovation at the end of this performance. People cannot help but stand, clap, and say, "Wow." ($$)

HOORAY FOR HOLLYWOOD

(Branson Variety Theater, 2701 W Hwy 76 ☎ 417.334.2500 ☋ bransonvarietytheatre.com) Musical lovers will thoroughly enjoy this nostalgic singing and dancing tribute to the last 50 years of Hollywood. There are performances from *Footloose*, *Grease*, Disney's *Beauty and the Beast*, *Mary Poppins*, *Singin' in the Rain* and *Saturday Night Fever*. There are even highlights from the movies including an appearance by Judy Garland singing "Somewhere Over the Rainbow." ($$)

IT ✪ Must See!

(3425 W. Hwy 76 ☎ 417.334.0076 ☋ hughes-brothers.com) "it" (with a lowercase "i") features an award winning cast of more than fifty dancers and musicians including the award winning Hughes Brothers and their ever-growing family. This is a squeaky-clean yet thoroughly entertaining family show filled with impeccable voices, precision dancing, and plenty of kids.

The Hughes Brothers have been a Branson favorite for years. Billed as the world's largest performing family, the Hughes Brothers act started with just Mom, Dad, and five boys. Now, "it" takes things to an entirely new level with impressive lighting and a wide range of music including pop, rock, country and gospel.

This is a squeaky-clean yet thoroughly entertaining family show filled with impeccable voices, precision dancing, popular songs, and plenty of kids. The intermission is almost as fun as the show— the brothers, youngest to oldest, toss flying saucer-shaped "balloons" all over the theater. "it" performs January through October. November 1st brings an equally impressive holiday show.

If Christmas is about kids, then the Hughes Brothers is where people should be during the holidays. This is one of the few performances in Branson to offer a full Christmas show. It seems every member of this large family has inherited true talent, including the adopted Russian siblings. There are violins, hand bells, dancing, glitzy costumes, even a live nativity. It's high energy yet perfectly sentimental. ($$)

KIRBY VANBURCH ✪ Must See!

(2353 Hwy 248 ☎ 417.337.7140 ⛉ kirbyvanburch.com) The princess of Thailand was so impressed with Kirby VanBurch that she gave him the title of "Prince of Magic." Kirby's mind-boggling show includes live white tigers, lions, a black panther, and VanBurch's signature illusion, a full-sized helicopter that appears in just three seconds. VanBurch has a particularly informal manner, with sometimes self-deprecating but good humor and a conversational style.

VanBurch's first experience with magic was at age seven, and at every show he chooses one young boy to assist him. Some of these kids have grown up to become performers in their own right, including magician Rob Lake. Another thing that sets this show apart is a telephone in the lobby that rings directly to Kirby VanBurch's dressing room. If guests encounter any problems, they are invited to pick up the phone. The magician promises to "make it right."

A backstage cat tour is available for an additional charge. This gives audience members the opportunity to have an up-close look at the feline stars of this magical show. ($$$)

PIERCE ARROW

(3069 Shepherd of the Hills Expy ☎ 417.336.8742
🖰 **piercearrowtheater.com)** Plenty of people swear by Pierce Arrow, saying it's the best show in town. Among these talented vocalists is the Guinness Book of World Records holder as the lowest bass singer. The music is a combination of country, patriotic, and gospel.

The musicians are backstage during the many comedic sketches. Audiences seem to love the hillbilly jokes offered. For those who want a blend of music and comedy, this is a good choice. ($)

PRESLEYS' COUNTRY JUBILEE

(2920 W Hwy 76 ☎ 417.334.4874 🖰 presleys.com) The Presleys: this family and its music play a big part in Branson's history. Long before the lights on the 76 Strip, the Presleys were enter-taining crowds in Missouri's natural theaters, the caves. When the crowds began overwhelming the caverns, the Presleys moved above ground and eventually became the first show on what would become Branson's famous Strip.

The Presleys' theater now is an enormous and comfortable showcase for 18 performing family members, not one of whom is related to Elvis. John Presley is fun and flirtatious from the piano. Other family members show up in flashy western costumes to sing classic country and gospel numbers. The stage is practically littered with guitars, banjos, drums, and any number of other instruments. During the Christmas season, the second half of the show is dedicated to holiday music.

Herkimer Presley, a favorite hillbilly for more than 45 years, is assigned to bring humor to the show. His son and protégé, Cecil, isn't much smarter. At the end of each performance it's almost shocking when these characters reveal their true—and normal—identities.

Before the show there's an old-fashioned gospel sing-along upstairs, where you can join in on classics like "The Old Rugged Cross," "Blessed Assurance," and "There is Power in the Blood." ($$)

Branson entertainment is a little like Branson's weather. It is always changing!

Educational Activities and Area Tours

Branson's variety is as evident in its attractions as in its music. Just about everyone can find something here that fits their interests and personality. There are extreme adventures, museums of all kinds, caves, wineries, and waterparks. Price ranges vary significantly according to the type of attraction. Designations using $=least expensive; $$=more expensive; $$$=most expensive are used to compare each type of attraction within this chapter.

AREA TOURS

Tours provide a variety of ways to experience the Branson area, each offering its own unique perspective. Visitors can see the Ozarks by boat, train, air, or even duck!

BRANSON BALLOON

(☎ 417.336.6060 ☋ bransonballoon.com) Soar above the Ozarks in the basket of a hot air balloon in a nearly four-hour excursion that starts with getting the balloon ready for takeoff. (Actual ride time is between one and two hours.)

Three people can ride at a time,with the option of two more in an additional balloon. Tours are given year-round if weather is favorable. Flights are by reservation only. A two-week advance notice is requested but not required. Flights take off just before sunrise or sunset for the most breathtaking views.

There are several launch sites depending on the customer's preference and wind direction. Staff provides transportation from accommodations to the launch site. ($$$)

MAIN STREET LAKE CRUISES

(7 N. Boardwalk ☎ 417.239.3980 🔗 mainstreetlakecruises.com) Groups or individuals can cruise Lake Taneycomo near downtown Branson on a paddleboat or a luxury yacht. Several different experiences are available, from an hour and a half of sightseeing to romantic dinner cruises and special holiday cruises. Tours also include a view of the Branson Landing fountains. Beverages and snacks are sold on board. ($$)

BRANSON SCENIC RAILWAY

(206 E Main St. ☎ 417.334.6110 🔗 bransontrain.com) From downtown Branson, a vintage train takes visitors on a nearly two-hour trip through the rolling Ozark landscape. Narrated stories describe various aspects of the railroad and the area. There's regular coach or glass dome seating, according to when tickets are purchased; there are no assigned seats. It's best to purchase as far in advance as possible. The glass dome seating upstairs offers the best view. Once on board, passengers are free to roam the train. There are concessions on each trip but be sure to have cash as credit cards cannot be accommodated while en route.

Some have complained that the word "scenic" is misleading. It's true that the view is mainly of brush and trees; don't expect wide expanses of picturesque landscape. This is mainly a relaxing train ride that goes about 20 miles outside of Branson and returns on the same track. Still, even the brush is pretty in the fall with its changing colors. This is the best time to expect any meaningful scenery.

In addition to the regular ride, a four-course candlelight dinner train experience is also available. And, during the holidays, families can enjoy a Polar Express experience. Kids wear their coziest pajamas and enjoy hot cocoa while listening to a reading of the Polar Express. Santa also makes an appearance during the trip. ($)

CHOPPER CHARTER

(Branson: 3005 W. Hwy 76 ☎ 417.332.1545; Hollister: 469 Blue Sky Ln ✆ choppercharter.com/branson_tours) For an entirely different way to see Branson, consider a helicopter tour. A wide range of prices and excursions is offered, or you can customize your own tour or simply get an airlift to various restaurants and shows. ($$$)

RIDE THE DUCKS

(2320 W. Hwy 76 & 150 Promenade Way ☎ 417.266.7600 ☎ 417.266.7655 ✆ ridetheducks.com) This is a great family experience. There are two tours available on these amphibious vehicles. The Table Rock Lake experience boards at Duck Central on Highway 76 (near Wal-Mart) for a quick tour of the entertainment district. Then drive down toward the dam that separates Table Rock and Taneycomo reservoirs, and splash into Table Rock for a tour of the lake. This is when the kiddos take charge. Get the cameras ready, because every child on board will have the opportunity to get in the driver's seat and steer the boat.

The Taneycomo experience leaves from Branson Landing (ticketing is next to Famous Dave's BBQ). Ride through historic downtown Branson as well as College of the Ozarks before splashing into Lake Taneycomo. This ride operates May through September.

Throughout the year there are different tour themes. If riding a boat-duck vehicle isn't awkward enough, try riding one decked out in lights and mistletoe during the holiday season! Half the fun is the captain who sings, tells jokes, and helps everyone get into the duck spirit. Tours last about an hour, with nearly half of that time spent on the water.

Be warned: The duck whistles are cute on the boat but obnoxious once vacation is over. It might be a good idea to "help" the kids lose them before a long drive home! Family pack discounts are available. ($)

SPIRIT OF AMERICA CRUISE
(State Park Marina, 380 State Park Marina Rd. ☎ 417.334.2628 📱 boatbranson.com) This 48-foot sailing catamaran offers a 90 minute sightseeing excursion and a two-hour Water World Adventure Cruise. This cruise stops in one of the lake's coves to allow guests an hour of water play on several large inflatables. Cruise times do change depending on weather. Up to 49 people can be accommodated on the Spirit of America. Snacks are available on board. ($)

CAVES AND CAVERNS

Missouri has been called "the cave state" because of the vast numbers of caverns carved into the limestone rock that makes up much of the landscape. Many are still undiscovered. There are more than 6,300 discovered caves, but only a handful of them are open to tourists. Those that are provide an inspiring look at this underground world.

It's been said that Jesse James and his gang used the Missouri caves to hide treasure and hide out. Caves were also used as hiding places during the Civil War. In addition to being used for shelter the caves have been utilized for growing mushrooms, storing food and drinks, even as entertainment venues. The largest cave entrance in the United States is found at Silver Dollar City's Marvel Cave.

Be sure kids are ready to experience the underground world. Caves, especially those with steep staircases to maneuver, can appear very intimidating for young children. The jeep-drawn tour of Fantastic Caverns is a nice introduction for hesitant little ones.

COSMIC CAVERN

(6386 Hwy 21 North Berryville, AR ☎ 870.749.2298
⬤ cosmiccavern.com) Less than an hour south of Branson (about half-way to Eureka Springs, Arkansas), Cosmic Cavern is the warmest cave in the Ozarks at 64° F year-round. The 96 percent humidity does make it feel a little warmer!

The unique features of this cave are its two so-called bottomless lakes, both seen on a tour that lasts just over an hour. Trout in one of the lakes have lost their color. The recently discovered Silent Splendor area contains a soda straw formation that measures nine feet long, one of the longest in the Ozarks. For people wanting more than a tour, Cosmic Cavern offers a caving experience with its after-hours Wild Cave Tour. Visit the website for information about the tour, which requires a 24-hour advance reservation. Gemstone panning is another activity offered here. Using an authentic sluice box, you can pan for a variety of gems and keep whatever you find. Check the website for coupons for cave tours. $

FANTASTIC CAVERNS

(4872 N. Farm Rd. 125, Springfield ☎ 417.833.2010
☀ fantasticcaverns.com) Twelve women answered an 1867 newspaper ad looking for explorers. That's how the first trailblazers came to venture into Fantastic Caverns, located just north of Springfield. The names of the women are still inscribed on the cave walls.

Today this is the only cave in America where visitors ride on a Jeep-tram throughout the hour-long tour. This makes it possible for those with small children and the physically impaired to take the tour. One of the first stops is the auditorium room, which used to host a live country music show. Guides talk about the cave's wildlife, its formation, and the importance of preservation. Visitors will enjoy the weather inside the cave no matter the time of year—it stays at an even 60° F year-round. ($$$)

TALKING ROCKS CAVERN

(423 Fairy Cave Lane, Branson West ☎ 417.272.3366
☀ talkingrockscavern.com) Talking Rocks Cavern was discovered in 1883 by a couple of boys who were rabbit hunting, but it wasn't until 1896 that explorer Truman Powell and five others actually ventured inside. When Silver Dollar City later bought the cave, it held a sound and light show inside, installing speakers to look like rocks. The cave was then named

Moonshine Beach *(© Julie Sedenko Davis)*

Branson Landing Cruises *(© Branson/Lakes Area Convention and Visitors Bureau)*

Table Rock Lake (© *Jay Kirschenmann*)

Murder Rock Golf Club *(© Murder Rock Golf Club)*

Big Cedar Lodge *(© Big Cedar Lodge)*

College of the Ozarks (© *College of the Ozarks*)

Old Matt's Cabin, Shepherd of the Hills *(© Julie Sedenko Davis)*

Dogwood Canyon Spirit Falls *(© Dogwood Canyon)*

Branson Belle and Chateau on the Lake *(© Branson/Lakes Area Convention and Visitors Bureau*

Butterfly Palace *(© Julie Sedenko Davis)*

Holiday Light Parade *(© Silver Dollar City)*

The Giant Swing *(© Silver Dollar City)*

Acrobats of China *(© Branson/Lakes Area Convention and Visitors Bureau)*

Talking Rocks. Experience just a little of what this show was like by taking a 40-minute tour of the cave.

There are thousands of natural formations in Talking Rocks Cavern. One is shaped like an angel, another like a fairy's harp. There's even a formation which resembles a small Mickey Mouse. Most impressive are the Cathedral Room and the 60-foot-tall Powell Column. There are about 150 stairs to maneuver inside the cave.

Beyond the cave tour, Talking Rocks offers mini-golf, nature trails, picnic facilities, gemstone mining, and two Speleobox mazes that allow people to experience what caving is like. ($$)

COLLEGE OF THE OZARKS ⊗ Must See!
(1 Opportunity Ave., Point Lookout ☎ 417.334.6411
🖱 cofo.edu) College of the Ozarks needs to be seen to be believed. Just a couple of miles south of Branson, its 1,000-acre Point Lookout site overlooks Lake Taneycomo. A tour of the campus is highly recommended for any visitor to the area.

The College of the Ozarks is practically drowning in accolades, including a listing as one of America's Best Colleges by *U.S. News and World Report.* It's not just the education that makes this school unique. It's also the price tag: most of its 1,400 students graduate debt free.

College of the Ozarks is one of seven working colleges in the United States. Students work 15 hours a week plus two 40-hour work weeks per semester to pay for their tuition.

Reverend James Forsyth founded the School of the Ozarks in 1906 to provide a Christian education for worthy underprivileged students. Changed to the College of the Ozarks in 1990, its stated mission is five-fold: academic, vocational, spiritual, patriotic, and cultural.

Point Lookout is a fully functioning and independent town. Students run pretty much everything, including the town's fire department, utilities, hospital, mill, greenhouses, dairy, and a world-famous fruitcake and jelly kitchen. In addition to a tractor museum, the Ralph Foster Museum is on campus and holds countless historical items pertaining to the Ozarks.

Visitors may take a free tour the college facilities, visit the museum, enjoy a meal at a student-run restaurant, and even stay overnight in the college's state-of-the-art Keeter Center. Student-guided tours are available for large groups. Others can check in with the public relations office and receive a campus map along with an audio CD. The CD gives an historical over-view of the school and explains the work program. Tours are offered year-round Monday through Friday from 9 a.m. to 4 p.m. Reservations are required. There is a small admission fee to the Ralph Foster Museum. Call ☎ 417.690.3241.

KEETER CENTER

(1 Opportunity Ave., Point Lookout ☎ 417.239.1900
🖱 keetercenter.edu) The professionalism and quality of this student-run facility at the College of the Ozarks are remark-able. The splendidly rustic lodge is a re-creation of Dobyns Hall, the Maine exhibition building brought here from the 1904 World's Fair in St. Louis. It was used as a hunting and fishing lodge until the school purchased the building, and it served the college until it burned down in 1930. Today Dobyns Hall has been resurrected in the form of the Keeter Center.

Keeter Center is where students learn hotel and restaurant management. It houses Dobyn's Dining, Mabee Lodge, the Beulah Winfrey Gift Shop, a gourmet bakery, conference rooms, and more.

MUSEUMS

There are a multitude of museums in the Branson area. From toys to the Titanic, Laura Ingalls Wilder's home to the Veteran's Memorial there is an almost endless amount of artifacts to keep everyone's interest. Prices are categorized as $=less expensive; $$=more expensive; $$$=most expensive.

BONNIEBROOK HISTORICAL SOCIETY

(485 Rose O'Neill Rd., Walnut Shade ☎ 417.561.1509

☗ roseoneill.org) Located just a few miles north of Branson off Highway 65, Bonniebrook is the former home of Rose O'Neill, artist and creator of the Kewpie doll. The 14-room mansion is a re-creation of the original home destroyed by fire in 1947, three years after her death. O'Neill named the original homestead Bonniebrook in 1894 for a stream that runs through the area. Bonniebrook was the first Taney County home with indoor plumbing, electricity, or a telephone.

Tours are given regularly throughout the week. During the Christmas season, Bonniebrook gets an old-fashioned holiday makeover. The museum is open April through November. Call or check the website for tour dates and times. ($)

DINOSAUR MUSEUM

(2020 W. Hwy 76 ☎ 417.335.8739 🖱 bransondinosaurs.com) A better name for this attraction might be "mini" museum. The small facility has five rooms filled with plastic dinosaur statues, including 13 full-sized figures and about a dozen dinosaur heads. In each room there is a television screen with a host describing facts about dinosaurs or the museum. At the end of the tour there is a small learning center complete with puzzles, books, coloring pages, and computers, all centered on dinosaurs. In the center of the museum and in the learning center, visitors can watch dinosaur-themed movies.

One word of warning for parents of little ones: the museum shares the building with the Haunted House & Monster Asylum. This means the screams from people touring the Haunted House can be heard inside the Dinosaur Museum. ($$)

HAROLD BELL WRIGHT MUSEUM

(World's Largest Toy Museum, 3609 W. Hwy 76 ☎ 417.332.1499 🖱 worldslargesttoymuseum.com) This museum is located inside the World's Largest Toy Museum, and the ticket price includes admission to both. Harold Bell Wright is responsible for much of the popularity Branson enjoys today. He put Branson on the map in many ways with the publication of his book *The Shepherd of the Hills*, which became a huge success. Inside the museum, visitors can see original handwritten manuscripts. Also on display is Wright's antique gun collection with weapons from the late 1800s.

Wright was also a minister, and his desire was that his books would impact people's lives. Wright's first book, *That Printer of*

Udell's, is said to have inspired an 11-year-old Ronald Reagan to become a Christian. A small wooden-pew theater inside the museum shows a film about Wright's life, writings, and ministry. ($$)

HOLLYWOOD WAX MUSEUM

(3030 W. Hwy 76 ☎ 417.337.8277 ◉ hollywoodwax.com) No one can miss the sight of King Kong scaling the outside of this building. Once inside, guests can have their picture taken in the grip of the oversized ape. (Of course, that will cost extra.) One of the best things about this museum is the chance to get up close and personal with the stars. A camera is a must, for pictures inside Jeannie's bottle, on the bench with Forrest Gump, even singing for the *American Idol* judges. Some like-nesses are great, while others could use touching up. Unless people are here for some fun photos, the museum doesn't take a lot of time. Because of this, some might find it overpriced for the experience. ($$$)

LAURA INGALLS WILDER HOME AND MUSEUM

(3068 Hwy A, Mansfield ☎ 877.924.7126 ◉ lauraingallswilderhome.com) Just over an hour northeast of Branson, this is the place where author Laura Ingalls Wilder and her husband, Almanzo, settled and raised their daughter, Rose. It's where all of the beloved "Little House" books were written. Located 45 miles east of Springfield, Laura's home is kept exactly as it was at the time of her death in 1957. Next door is a Laura Ingalls Wilder–Rose Wilder Lane museum containing handwritten manuscripts, artifacts belonging to Laura and her family, even needlework done by the author.

Perhaps most important is Pa's fiddle, the actual one he played during her childhood.

Another section of the museum features writings and artifacts from daughter Rose Wilder Lane. The rock house Rose built for her parents is also part of the tour. No picture-taking is allowed in either home, but postcards are available in the gift shop. Laura, Almanzo, and Rose are buried on the property in a cemetery that you can also visit.

Visitors in the area in September may be interested in attending Mansfield's annual Laura Ingalls Wilder festival, always held on the third Saturday in September. ($)

RALPH FOSTER MUSEUM

**(College of the Ozarks, 1 Opportunity Ave, Hollister
☎ 417.334.6411 ☋ rfostermuseum.com)** One of the favorite items on display here is the 1921 Oldsmobile featured in the television series *The Beverly Hillbillies*. Paul Henning, the producer of the show, was from this area and donated the vehicle. *The Beverly Hillbillies* actually shot several episodes at Branson's Silver Dollar City.

The Ralph Foster Museum was originally named the Museum of the Ozarks, which describes its purpose well. All things Ozarks are preserved and cherished here. The museum was later named after a local radio pioneer and avid outdoorsman who collected Indian artifacts. His vast collection was donated to the museum that now bears his name.

The museum has undergone several expansions. The three-story building now contains more than 40,000 square feet of exhibit space as well as a research library. Among the exhibits is a large collection of Kewpie dolls, a nod to early local artist Rose O'Neill, who created them. There's an impressive display of guns, including a rifle owned by Pancho Villa. Local celebrities including writer Harold Bell Wright and such tourism pioneers as the Herschend, Presley, and Mabe families are honored here. Also on display are furniture, toys, and stuffed animals of every size. At some times, students run a hands-on program for kids, and a Children's Discovery Room has interactive displays about the solar system, time zones, and more. ($)

RIPLEY'S BELIEVE IT OR NOT

(3326 W. Hwy 76 ☎ 417.337.5300 🖰 ripleysbranson.com) You can't miss Ripley's on the Strip—it's the house with the huge crack down the middle. The reason for this architectural peculiarity is to illustrate the worst earthquake on record. It happened, not in California, but in New Madrid, Missouri. The earthquake registered 8.0 on the Richter scale and was so intense that it rang church bells in Philadelphia and caused the Mississippi River to run backwards for three days. These are just some of the facts revealed during a self-guided Ripley's tour. There are hundreds of exhibits, including a human unicorn, a two-headed calf, statues of the world's tallest man, a Roman coliseum made of playing cards, and a gallery of illusions. ($$$)

TITANIC MUSEUM ⭐ Must See!

(3235 W. Hwy 76 ☎ 417.334.9500 🖰 titanicbranson.com) The Titanic sits in the center of the Branson strip looking ominous and impressive. Walk into this ship-shaped museum—built to half the scale of the original Titanic—and assume the identity of one of the actual ship passengers as you're given a boarding pass with his or her name. Throughout the self-guided tour, staff members dressed in period costumes tell true stories about the individual named on your boarding pass.

The interactive features of the museum are outstanding. Walk the elegant replica of the ship's grand staircase, hear the captain's voice while standing on the bridge, and explore the cabins in each class. Step outside to see the infamous mountain of ice that ripped through the gargantuan boat, and even touch the iceberg to feel how cold it was. Sit in a lifeboat and hear other survivors talk, then experience what it was like for those who didn't get in the lifeboats by slipping a hand into 28-degree water and leaving it there as long as possible.

There are 20 rooms inside the Titanic Museum, each holding a different experience and together containing 400 artifacts relating to passengers or crew members. Perhaps the most chilling moment is finding "your" name on a list of who lived and who died—largely determined by the class of the ticket.

The Titanic hosts a number of special events throughout the year, many to honor those who lost their lives and to tell the stories of those who survived. A new gallery will pay tribute to one of the Titanic's most infamous survivors, the "Unsinkable Molly Brown." Other events include mother-daughter teas, youth nights, chili cook-off's, and even Irish-themed occasions. Christmas is always beautiful aboard the Titanic with impressive decorations and special holiday happenings. Check the website for the latest calendar of events. Family passes are available and include two adults and up to four children. ($$$)

TRACTOR MUSEUM

(College of the Ozarks, 1 Opportunity Ave, Point Lookout
☎ 417.334.6411 ☋ cofo.edu) This small museum contains about a dozen antique tractors, some of which still run. See a 1919 Massey-Harris and a 1935 John Deere B as well as tractor parts and machinery. The museum is part of the College of the Ozarks tour. There is no admission to this museum but campus tour reservations are required.

VETERAN'S MEMORIAL MUSEUM

(1250 W. Hwy 76 ☎ 417.336.2300
☋ veteransmemorialbranson.com) The entertainers and citizens of Branson mean business when it comes to paying tribute to the men and women who serve this country in the military. Probably the ultimate tribute comes at this museum, which offers a moving experience that begins with the full-sized WWII P-51 Mustang fighter in the parking lot.

The focus on personal stories and memorabilia sets this experience apart. The world's largest war memorial bronze sculpture is here, depicting soldiers storming a beachfront. The life-sized figures were sculpted after actual men from each state. World-renowned sculptor Fred Hoppe, himself a veteran, is responsible for the impressive tribute and for the museum itself. Inside the museum are thousands of war-torn fragments of history. The personal impact is everywhere, including the walls of the museum. Written on them are the names of those killed in World War II and every conflict since then—the only place in the world the names are displayed together.

The self-guided tour takes visitors into separate rooms dedicated to each 20th-century conflict. There are stories of individual acts of bravery and loss, and personal items that saved lives or took them. The World War II room displays Nazi artifacts such as Hitler's WWI dog tag and his partner Eva Braun's pistol and tea set, along with gas masks, Japanese Kamikaze uniforms, and other chilling pieces of the past. ($$$)

WILSON'S CREEK BATTLEFIELD

(6424 W Farm Rd. 182, Republic ☎ 417.732.2662 ♉ wilsonscreek.com) About an hour's drive north from Branson is the site of the first major battle of the Civil War in the West. Nearly a quarter of the Union Army was killed, wounded, or captured here on August 10, 1861. The Confederacy lost 12 percent of its army. Altogether there were 1,700 casualties at what came to be known as Bloody Hill. This was the beginning of more than four years of fighting in Missouri.

Wilson's Creek Battlefield, operated as part of the National Park System, is now home to a Civil War museum and a research library. The park also includes the Ray House, where farmer and postmaster John Ray lived with his family during the fight, and the restored Edwards Cabin, site of Confederate General Sterling Price's headquarters. A fiber optic map and interpretive film help visitors understand the reality of the battle. Wilson's Creek holds a number of special events throughout the year. ($)

WORLD'S LARGEST TOY MUSEUM

(3609 W. Hwy 76 ☎ 417.332.1499 ♉ worldslargesttoymuseum. com) Relive childhood memories with this museum's collection dating from the 1800s to today, from tractors and trains and cowboy memorabilia to Shirley Temple and Kewpie dolls. You'll find everything from Star Wars to Howdy Doody, Power

Rangers to Popeye. Also located inside the World's Largest Toy Museum is a museum focused on Harold Bell Wright, author of The Shepherd of the Hills. Admission to both is included in the ticket price. ($$)

NATURE TOURS AND ATTRACTIONS

One of the main draws to Branson is its natural surroundings. These experiences allow visitors the opportunity to get up close and personal with nature and learn a little about the Ozarks.

THE BUTTERFLY PALACE & RAINFOREST ADVENTURE
(4106 W. Hwy 76 ☎ 417.332.2231 ● thebutterflypalace.com)
This is a photo enthusiast's dream. Almost 200 species of butterflies from around the world flutter away inside a carefully controlled rainforest environment. You can get as close as you want, and some butterflies may even come to you. Kids can put on real pith helmets and magnify the view with child-sized binoculars. Other attractions inside the Palace include the Emerald Forest Mirror Maze and a small science center where kids can experience more rainforest creatures. Outside, kids and adults alike can don harnesses and climb a faux coconut tree.

At some times of the year the rainforest offers a glowing night-time experience. During the Christmas season, visitors listen to holiday music while watching white butterflies fly among twinkling lights, seasonal flowers, and living angel statues.

This attraction is not for thrill seekers. The butterfly portion is basically a large atrium filled with vegetation and butterflies.

Some will love being so close to these creatures; others may be bored. ($$$)

SHEPHERD OF THE HILLS FISH HATCHERY ✪ Must See!
(483 Hatchery Rd. ☎ 417.334.4865
🖱 mdc.mo.gov/regions/southwest/shepherd-hills-fish-hatchery)
One of the things people love about this fish hatchery next to Table Rock Dam is the admission price: free. There are thousands of brown and rainbow trout swimming in huge holding areas here, just waiting to be fed. Food costs a quarter, well worth it for the show as fish vie for a bite. Ask at the front for a cup to hold the food, or bring your own.

Guided tours are regularly available from Memorial Day to Labor Day, after which tours are self-guided. Visitors see fish in every cycle of life, beginning with the egg incubation period. Along with movies and exhibits about fish, the visitor center includes various reptiles and spiders native to Missouri. This stop makes an entertaining learning experience for the entire family.

TABLE ROCK DAM/DEWEY SHORT VISITORS CENTER
(4600 Hwy 165 ☎ 417.334.6394 🖱 tablerockdamtours.com) This is a nice fact-finding and adventure stop. The visitor center has all kinds of information about Table Rock Lake and the Ozarks, including an exhibit on the area's natural history and how Table Rock Dam was built. The Discovery Shop gift store offers educational toys and products focusing on wildlife and water preservation, along with local artwork. The beginning of the 2.2-mile Table Rock Lakeshore Trail is here. It is suitable for wheelchairs and strollers, as it is level and nicely paved.

Educational Activities

For the adventure side of things, visitors can purchase a ticket to peek inside the concrete Table Rock dam, completed in 1958 to control flooding. A refurbished San Francisco cable car takes visitors to the powerhouse to begin the walking tour which lasts just over an hour. Tour members must be American citizens, and those 16 and older should be prepared to show photo identification. For safety reasons, children less than six years old are not allowed on the tour. ($$)

SHEPHERD OF THE HILLS HOMESTEAD ⭐ Must See!

(5586 W. Hwy 76 ☎ 417.334.4191 🌐 oldmatt.com) For anyone who wants to understand Branson's history, the Shepherd of the Hills Homestead is a must. Located just a few miles from downtown, this homestead started it all. A guided tour gives a well-rounded look at the homestead site. It includes stops at Old Matt's Cabin, Inspiration Point, Morgan Community Church, Old Matt's grist mill, and the Old Mill Theatre. The tour ends at Jenning's Still for a memorable lesson in making moonshine.

Several shows are performed at the Shepherd of the Hills. This is also the location of the Vigilante Extreme ZipRider experience. Attractions and entertainment can be purchased separately or together in a discounted combo ticket. ($-$$$)

INSPIRATION TOWER

This 230-foot-tall structure is a Branson landmark built on an already famous landmark, the homestead of John and Anna Ross. This couple is also known as Old Matt and Aunt Molly from the book *The Shepherd of the Hills*.

A glass elevator takes you to the top for a panoramic view of the Ozarks landscape—as far as 90 miles on a clear day. Autumn offers especially colorful views. During the Christmas season, Inspiration Tower is the starting point for the popular Trail of Lights. ($)

OLD MATT'S CABIN

This cabin was standing in the Ozark Mountains long before any theaters or theme parks existed. A simple pioneer home in what was then wilderness, it was where a traveling preacher named Harold Bell Wright, suffering from ill health, went to recuperate in 1896. That summer-long visit (and several more to follow) resulted in Wright's best-selling novel *The Shepherd of the Hills*, credited with sparking the beginning of tourism in the area.

Today the small wood cabin is recorded in the National Register of Historic Places. Visitors can take a jeep-drawn tram tour and see inside the meager accommodation that was home to John and Anna Ross, the gracious strangers who opened their cabin to Wright. Also on the hour-long tour is Little Pete's cave (mentioned in Wright's book), the grounds of Inspiration Point and a behind-the-scenes look at the Shepherd of the Hills outdoor drama. Combination prices are available for those wanting to experience more than one of the attractions at Shepherd of the Hills. ($$)

MORGAN COMMUNITY CHURCH

This church sits on the homestead property to show the kind of buildings in which Harold Bell Wright ministered. This particular church was built in 1901 in Morgan, Missouri, about

80 miles northeast of Branson. It was saved from demolition with its relocation to the Shepherd of the Hills homestead.

WINERIES

Several award-winning wineries are located in Branson. Two offer free tours and all offer free wine tasting.

BRANSON RIDGE WINERY

(307 Branson Landing Blvd. ☎ 417.335.9700

⬤ bransonridgewinery.com) The Branson Ridge Winery is the newest in the area. It does not offer tours, but you can taste the wine for a fee. You can also create your own wine label, branding the bottle with your name or personalizing it as a gift. Located at the Branson Landing shopping center, Branson Ridge also operates the Cafe diVine. The cafe's covered patio provides a nice environment for enjoying the Landing's atmosphere. Menu items include soups, paninis, cheeses, and desserts.

MOUNT PLEASANT WINERY

(3125 Green Mountain Dr. ☎ 417.336.9463

⬤ mountpleasant.com) A German immigrant began Mount Pleasant Winery in 1859 in the town of Augusta, near St. Louis. The winery grows 16 different types of grapes there on more than 85 acres, but Mount Pleasant also has a winery of more than 9,000 square feet in Branson. Visitors can tour and taste wine free of charge and even bottle their own dessert wine from a 600-gallon French oak barrel. Local artwork is on display at the winery.

Educational Activities

Mount Pleasant recently established a bottle recycling program. Anyone bringing a bottle from any winery for recycling will receive ten percent off any take-home purchase.

STONE HILL WINERY

(601 Hwy 165 ☎ 417.334.1897 ☗ stonehillwinery.com) The Stone Hill Winery is one of the oldest and largest wineries in the country. Started by German immigrants in 1847 in Hermann, Missouri, it remains a family-owned business to this day. Company headquarters are still in Hermann, near St. Louis, but now the winery has several other locations as well. Branson is where Stone Hill makes its unique baked cream sherry along with its Golden Spumonte and blush wines.

A free one-hour tour includes a brief history of the winery as well as tasting of various Stone Hill wines, including the baked cream sherry, dry vignoles, Steinberg white, and others. Tours leave from the lobby and gift area frequently. Those 35 and under will need to show identification to take part in the tasting. Kids may sample sparkling juices.

Educational Activities

Just for Fun

Whether zipping through the Ozark landscape, cooling off at a waterpark or simply taking in a movie, these attractions are what vacations are about: fun! Price designations are compared within each section. $=less expensive; $$=more expensive; $$$=most expensive.

EXTREME ADVENTURES

Those who love an adrenaline rush will relish these attractions. Some offer a quick thrill while others, like the Branson Zipline & Canopy Tours, have the option of spending hours zipping through the Ozark treetops.

ADVENTURE ZIPLINES OF BRANSON
(501 N. Wildwood Dr. ☎ 417.239.3030

📱 adventureziplinesofbranson.com) Adventurers can fly through the air over the Sevierville forest canopy right in the heart of Branson, reaching speeds of 50 mph while attached to a stainless-steel cable. There are six different rides of varying lengths and heights, with an option to zip at night. This is one of the most economical zipline experiences in the area, and discounts are offered; call or check the website. Tips for the guides are not included in the ticket price.

There is a spiral staircase to climb to get to the zipline, and there are three short walk-bridges to traverse. ($$)

BRANSON BALLKNOCKER

(3330 W Harvey Dr. ☎ 417.335.3958 🖱 ballknocker.com) Picture a 12-foot clear ball with a six-foot inner chamber surrounded by a cushion of air. Now picture being harnessed into that chamber with a couple of friends and being launched down a hill. Not enough adrenaline? Try the Branson Wet Ballknocker. No harnesses here, just you, friends, the ball, and gallons of water going in circles down a 550-foot run. These are quick but extreme rides for those looking for a unique thrill. ($)

BRANSON ZIPLINE & CANOPY TOURS

(Wolf Creek Preserve, 2339 Hwy 65, Walnut Shade ☎ 800.712.4654 🖱 bransonzipline.com) It's extreme but, really, safe for all ages! Zipline & Canopy Tours even offers a discount for folks ages 62 and above. The only requirements are to be within 70 and 275 pounds and to meet general health standards.

Of several tour options, the Ozarks Xplorer Canopy Tour is the longest, with 2 ½ hours of suspension bridges, ziplines, and unparalleled views of the Ozarks landscape.

The shortest is a quick thrill ride on the Blue Streak Fast Line. The worst—or best—part is disembarking from a 100-foot tower back to ground level. A completely different experience is offered at night. Branson Zipline and Canopy tours is located ten minutes north of Branson off Highway 65. ($$-$$$)

VIGILANTE EXTREME ZIPRIDER

(The Shepherd of the Hills, 5586 W. Hwy 76 ☎ 800.653.6288 🖱 oldmatt.com) This is a little different from a zip line, because

Just for Fun

people are seated and need to do absolutely nothing to enjoy the ride. They don't even need to hang on. Speed control and braking are automatic, so it's an effortless ride to the bottom.

The ZipRider claims to have the highest launch point in the world at 170 feet above ground. From there it propels riders half a mile down a length of steel cable at up to 50 mph. It may seem scary, but the ride to the bottom is fast enough to be fun without being terrifying. At Christmas the night ride offers a nice view of the Trail of Lights. ($)

MOVIE THEATERS

Even with all of the live stage shows in Branson there is still room for the silver screen. Enjoy a regular theatre or choose from plush seating at the Elite Cinema and even a mega-sized movie at the IMAX.

BRANSON MEADOWS CINEMAS
(4740 Gretna Rd. ☎ 417.332.0464
🖱 bransonmeadowscinema11.com) The Branson Meadows Cinemas 11 offers the latest box office movies. They also occasionally have 3D movies which cost a bit more than the usual ticket price. ($$)

ELITE CINEMA III
(3562 Shepherd of the Hills Expy ☎ 800.419.4832
🖱 bransonimax.com) This cinema features three theaters with stadium seating and digital surround sound. Oversized seats are luxurious with Tempur-pedic foam padding, adjustable arm

rests and plenty of leg room. Check the website for discount coupons. ($)

GIANT-SCREEN IMAX ADVENTURES
(3562 Shepherd of the Hills Expy ☎ 800.419.4832
⛾ bransonimax.com) This is the ultimate cinema experience with a screen six stories high and wrap-around digital sound. Shows include box office movies as well as special IMAX adventure experiences which might be undersea mysteries, a Lewis and Clark expedition or the local historical film, Ozarks Legacy and Legend. Call or go online for the latest shows and times. ($$)

HAUNTED EXPERIENCES

No one need wait for Halloween to go through a haunted house. These frightening attractions are open all year.

CASTLE OF CHAOS
(3030 W. Hwy 76 ☎ 417.337.8700
⛾ castleofchaosbranson.com) Billed as the world's first 5D interactive haunted experience, this is part horror film, part video game, and part thrill ride. It takes place in what is supposed to be a Belgian castle, where fictitious horror film star Carli Winnipeg was last seen while filming the fictitious movie "Castle of Chaos." Guests are seated on a platform of theater seats that spins quickly in 180-degree turns from one scene to the next throughout the ride, which lasts less than ten minutes. There are pretend guns for guests to use to fight the "evil," but it's unclear exactly where to shoot. At times a blast of air may give an extra startle.

There is a lot of movement in the ride, which could cause motion sickness. The 3D effects are somewhat disappointing. Overall, it's a unique experience but seems overpriced for the very short time it takes. There is a lower price for kids 11 and under, but this is not appropriate for younger children. ($$)

HAUNTED HOUSE AND MONSTER ASYLUM

(2020 W. Hwy 76 ☎ 417.334.2868 🎧 hauntedinbranson.com)
This is definitely an adult experience, too scary for little ones. Without giving too much of the experience away, rest assured there are things inside this "house" that will make a person jump. There are clowns—probably enough said—and some animatronics that can be a bit spooky. Be prepared for the gory side of horror, too. There is the option of going through the Haunted House with or without actors. Both ways are scary, but the actors will keep people jumping and lend an eerie feeling that likely will follow guests home. A discount ticket combination ticket, which includes the Dinosaur Museum, is available. ($$)

TRACK FAMILY FUN PARKS

(2505 W. Hwy 76; 3345 W. Hwy 76; 3525 W Hwy 76; 2911 Green Mountain Dr. ☎ 417.334.1612 🎧 bransontracks.com) There are several of these activity-packed parks throughout Branson. All include various combinations of bumper boats, sky coasters, bumper cars, go-karts, laser tag, miniature golf, and arcade games, making them fun places for adults to let loose and compete with the kids in some serious playtime. Special birthday rooms make this a popular place for a party; check the website for discount pricing. ($-$$)

WATERPARKS

There are several fun places in Branson to cool off in the hot summer months. The biggest waterpark, White Water, is located on the east end of the strip. Two others, while part of resort accommodations, are open to the public.

CASTLE ROCK RESORT AND WATERPARK

(3001 Green Mountain Dr. ☎ 417.336.6000

🖱 castlerockbranson.com) Day tickets to this waterpark are available. See the "Lodging" section for information about this resort. ($$)

SPLASH COUNTRY WATERPARK RESORT

(1945 W. Hwy 76 ☎ 417.335.3535 🖱 grandcountry.com) This waterpark is part of the Grand Country Resort on 76 strip. Admission is included for guests of the resort but can also be purchased by those not staying at the property.

This small but impressive indoor waterpark is like a giant obstacle course. Kids (and parents) climb ropes and cross bridges to reach two giant slides. But watch out—others are taking aim with giant soaker guns that can blast unsuspecting targets. Also listen for the bell warning that an avalanche of water is about to be dumped from a massive bucket atop a two-story play structure.

Lazy River offers a more leisurely experience. There are also two very large hot tubs, one of them set to a temperature more like bathwater so kids can relax with their parents. Even infants will enjoy mini slides, spouts, and baby swings hanging just above very shallow water. For those not looking for the action of a waterpark, there are two outdoor pools and an indoor heated pool and spa. ($$)

WHITE WATER

(3505 W. Hwy 76 ☎ 417.336.7100 ⬤ bransonwhitewater.com)
Branson's only outdoor waterpark, White Water has 12 acres of rides. There are high-speed slides for those looking for an adrenalin rush, plenty of options for the little ones, and a lazy river for those just wanting to relax and cool off. There's also a sand volleyball court inside the park. Cabanas are available to rent in various sizes for families or groups; reservations must be made in advance. Life jackets and inner tubes are provided free of charge. White Water is open from the end of May through early September. Check the website for a detailed schedule and special pricing.

Aloha River. White Water recently enjoyed a big expansion with the addition of Aloha River at Hula Hula Bay. This Polynesian jungle–themed attraction can be drenching or more relaxing, depending on the your mood. The waters are calm, but there are unexpected twists, fountains, and misters. It's the longest ride in the park at 800 feet. Seating and cabanas are available along the way.

Kalani Towers. The ultimate thrill slide at White Water is the Kalani Towers. There are two options here: the Tower Racer or the Speed Slide. You can choose to freefall 75 feet and then body surf at up to 40 mph for the rest of the 300-foot drop, or you can slide on mats 312 feet at more than 25 mph. There are several lanes on the slide, so people can race each other to the bottom.

Just for Fun

Rain Tree Island. Rain Tree Island has 20,000 square feet of aqua-shooters, geysers, and slides. Look up, or you might get hit when the 700-gallon RainTree bucket tips over.

Surfquake Wave Pool. This 500,000-gallon adventure may look tame as people swim and play, but when the bell rings, get ready for the wave. This is a blast for tubing or body-surfing. ($$$).

Just for Fun

Lodging

There is no shortage of places to stay in the Branson area. In fact, there are 22,000 hotel rooms, in accommodations that range from economy hotels on the Strip to national chains or romantic bed and breakfast inns. Those on a budget may want to consider listening to a condominium sales presentation in order to receive a free stay in a top-of-the-line condo.

A number of hotels, resorts, and campgrounds welcome pets. See the individual listings for information on each of the facilities listed below. For assistance in locating pet-friendly Branson lodging, visit the website ● petswelcome.com.

Following a select listing of B&Bs, hotels are categorized by location. This is by no means a comprehensive list, but it does contain a variety of options in different areas and at different price points.

Prices for lodging are categorized $=least expensive, $$=more expensive and $$$=most expensive. These categories reflect price but not necessarily value. Even though an accommodation's actual price may be higher it may still be a better value when considering free meals, amenities and inclusive activities.

BED AND BREAKFAST INNS

Bed and breakfast inns are a popular choice among travelers for many reasons. They are personal, romantic, usually historical, and thoroughly unique. All of the following come with the author's personal recommendation. There are no shared bathrooms, and if you're a late riser or desire a more privacy, Aunt Sadie's offers a light breakfast in your room.

ANCHOR INN ON THE LAKE ⊕ Must See!
(100 Hurtville Lane, Branson West ☎ 877.307.9140 📱 anchorinnonthelake.com) For those looking for a special place for a honeymoon or an anniversary celebration, this is it. This beautiful inn sits on Table Rock Lake just a short drive through the countryside west of Branson. After being greeted by owners Mike and Dee and enjoying Dee's homemade cookies, guests are escorted to one of four exquisitely decorated rooms. The entire inn has a nautical theme (a nod to Mike's career in the Navy), and each guest room is named after a place where the couple has lived. Gas fireplaces and two-person Jacuzzi tubs make the rooms mini-retreats. Candlelit bubble bath and instrumental CDs set a romantic mood. Specialized packages can be ordered to make stays even more memorable. ($$-$$$)

AUNT SADIE'S BED AND BREAKFAST
(163 Fountain St. ☎ 417.335.4063 📱 auntsadies.com) Aunt Sadie's is the perfect compromise when one partner doesn't want to get up early for breakfast and the other wants the quaint, romantic inn experience. Homemade pastries, cereals, fruit, and other snacks are served in the evening so that couples can wake up and eat on their own schedule.

The location is wooded and private yet just 5 miles from town, with easy access to the back roads around the Branson Strip. Each of the five separate cottages has its own deck and hot tub, and several also have large, in-room Jacuzzi tubs. Fireplaces, mini-refrigerators, microwaves, and coffeemakers are among the amenities. Aunt Sadie's is a fine choice for a romantic stay or a girlfriends'retreat; special packages are available, and spa treatments are offered at an extra charge. ($$$)

THE BRANSON HOUSE
(120 North 4th St ☎ 417.838.8880 🖱 thebransonhouse.com)

Guys won't have to turn in their "man-card" when checking into The Branson House near downtown's Branson Landing. Owner Dale Coursey is proud to announce there are no doilies, antiques or scented soaps in his newly remodeled bed and breakfast. This is a place where men can relax on leather couches and enjoy a filling (but not frilly) breakfast.

Still, romance is alive and well at The Branson House. Flowers, cupcakes, in-room massages, show tickets and more can be added to make your stay personal and memorable. There are five rooms at The Branson House. Among them is the honeymoon suite featuring a two-person jacuzzi tub and a wet bar with wine cooler.

The Branson House has an interesting history. Jim Owen, mayor of Branson before there were the Presley's or Baldknobbers, once owned this property. Back then dancing was banned and lawbreakers were fined. Owen was a fishing guide for many famous people including President Truman and a number of congressmen. One of his fishing clients, Charlton Heston, is said to have stayed here.

A Branson House breakfast is usually derived from a family recipe. Dale focuses on country style meals like French toast with eggs and bacon, breakfast burritos, biscuits and gravy or ham and eggs. ($$)

Lodging

BRADFORD INN

(3590 Hwy 265 ☎ 417.338.5555 🖱 bradfordinn.us) This New England–style inn is situated just a few minutes away from town, but the surrounding trees make it feel more rural. There are 33 themed rooms, some of them connecting for family convenience. The themes vary greatly, from highly decorated to simple. Smaller rooms have queen beds, sleeper sofa, and refrigerator. Others also have Jacuzzi tubs. There is a honeymoon suite, and there's even a townhouse that has a full kitchen, living room with fireplace, and two full baths.

Breakfast, included in the room rate, is made to order by the owner and includes waffles, eggs, sausage, biscuits and gravy, coffee cake, fruit, and beverages. Lunch is available for purchase in the dining area Wednesday through Saturday and features pizza, sandwiches, homemade soups, and salads. Everything is made from scratch. ($-$$)

CRYSTAL COVE CABINS

(635 Compton Ridge Rd ☎ 417.338.2715 🖱 crystalcovebranson.com) This rustic retreat is hidden in a quiet mountainside next to Table Rock Lake. The grounds include lush landscaping and waterfalls along with a private boat dock, hiking trails and a campfire area. While secluded, Crystal Cove Cabins is convenient to Branson…just a five-minute drive to Silver Dollar City.

Luxury log cabins set a romantic mood with comfortable, king-sized log beds, two-person Jacuzzis and fireplaces. Other amenities include 37-inch flat screen televisions and kitchenettes.

Lodging

Guests enjoy gourmet breakfasts in a beautiful dining room overlooking a waterfall and Koi gardens. Satisfying meals include apple cinnamon French toast, biscuits and gravy, eggs Benedict, cinnamon rolls and more. ($$-$$$)

BRANSON LANDING/DOWNTOWN BRANSON

Downtown Branson has the feel of an older time, with its 5 & 10 store, ice cream parlors, and old-fashioned buildings. Hiding around the corner is a modern outdoor shopping mall, Branson Landing, which brings shopping, shows, and lakefront dining. There's even a Starbucks within walking distance. The Branson Scenic Railway station is across the street at the convention center.

BEST WESTERN LANDING VIEW INN & SUITES

(403 W Hwy 76 ☎ 877.368.3782 ⬥ bwlandingview.com) Within walking distance of Branson Landing, this hotel gives guests a nice value with its many complimentary amenities. Children under 18 stay free. High-speed Internet is free. A deluxe continental breakfast comes with the price of a room. The fireplace in the breakfast lounge is soothing in the colder months.

Room amenities include flat screen televisions, refrigerators, microwaves, and coffeemakers. There are also Jacuzzi suites available. Hotel facilities include a playground, a game room, an indoor pool with sliding glass doors that can be opened during the summer months, and an outdoor hot tub. ($$)

Lodging

HILTON CONVENTION CENTER

(200 E Main St. ☎ 417.336.5400 📞 hilton.com) Right across the street from Branson Landing, the Hilton Convention Center gives a striking first impression with its contemporary lobby. Rooms are spacious and inviting, with marble counters and modern decor. Amenities include refrigerators, coffeemakers, and robes. A good night's sleep is easy to come by with the plush pillows and comfortable mattresses.

The hotel has a fitness room, an indoor pool, and a hot tub. There is a cocktail lounge, and the Level 2 Steakhouse is open for breakfast, lunch, and dinner. There's a hefty per-day charge for parking and another charge for Internet access. ($$$)

HILTON PROMENADE ON THE LANDING

(3 Branson Landing Blvd. ☎ 417.336.5500 📞 hilton.com) Shopping is just an elevator ride away at the Hilton Promenade. This hotel is part of Branson Landing and offers plush rooms and amenities. Beds have pillow-topped mattresses and down comforters, and rooms feature 32-inch flat screen televisions, mini-refrigerators, microwaves, and coffeemakers. In addition to regular hotel rooms, this facility offers suites and even condos. Some rooms have walk-in showers and no tubs; some even have washers and dryers.

The indoor pool and heated whirlpool are top quality. A fitness center is also available. The only downside is the extra charges for parking and Internet use. ($$$)

LANDMARK INN

(315 N Commercial St. ☎ 417.334.1304 📞 landmarkinnbranson.com) This turn-of-the-century building

Lodging

was originally home to the railroad stationmaster, later becoming a boarding house. Today it is a quaint eight-room hotel that's a reasonably priced choice for anyone wanting to be close to downtown. The Landmark is across the street from Branson Landing. In the warmer months guests can enjoy the pool or the home's large decks and bench swing. Rooms include a coffeepot, a microwave, and a small refrigerator. ($)

GREEN MOUNTAIN DR./THOUSAND HILLS AREA

This area in the central part of town is close to shopping, shows, and dining. It's near the Andy Williams Moon River Theatre, miniature golf, and both Mount Pleasant and Stone Hill wineries.

CASTLE ROCK RESORT AND WATERPARK
(3001 Green Mountain Dr. ☎ 417.336.6000
🖱 **castlerockbranson.com)** This resort has 200 guest rooms and an indoor waterpark. The main draw, of course, is the waterpark; admission is included in the price of the room. Day passes can also be purchased by those not staying at the hotel. The park has a large corkscrew slide and a 30-foot tube slide as well as a lazy river and kiddie slides. In the warmer months an outdoor wading pool is available.

Rooms are not fancy, but they are unique and designed with kids in mind. Each has as "kiddie cove" with bunk beds and a flat screen television. Microwaves and refrigerators are available for a small fee. Suites and atrium rooms are also available; the atrium rooms do not have the kiddie coves, and guests must walk outside to gain access to the park. The Tower Grill serves breakfast, lunch, and dinner. Kids' menus are available, and prices are reasonable. ($$)

GRAND CROWNE RESORT

(300 Golfview Dr. ☎ 800.313.8530 🖱 grandcrowneresorts.com)
This large condominium resort is nestled into the trees just
blocks away from the Strip. The property and its parking
lot may feel imposing from the outside, but the rooms are
comfortable and homey-feeling. Options range from a one-
bedroom standard to a three-bedroom premier condo. Even
the least expensive option features microwave, refrigerator,
washer and dryer, sleeper sofa, and private bedroom. Upgrades
include a full kitchen with dishwasher, a great room, a dining
area, and a deck.

Unique to this property is a Veterans Memorial Room, housing
a large quantity of donated war memorabilia. There's no charge
to see the room, and it's worth the time to take a look. Other
amenities include an activities room with various things going
on for kids; facilities for basketball, volleyball, badminton, and
tennis; a children's playground; a small game room; a fitness
center; and a clubhouse pavilion.

These condos offer good value, and if more than one family
shares a condo the price is even more reasonable. Furry family
members are also welcome in designated pet units. ($$-$$$)

THE STONE CASTLE HOTEL AND CONFERENCE CENTER

**(3050 Green Mountain Dr. ☎ 800.677.6906
🖱 stonecastlehotel.com)** The outside of this 300-room hotel
is impressive, with its castle-like architecture. Inside, the guest
rooms are clean and comfortable, including such amenities as
refrigerators and microwaves, coffeemakers, hair dryers, and
free Wi-Fi. All rooms open to an indoor hallway. The hotel

Lodging

and furnishings are not brand new, and it shows in minor ways; there may be small scratches on the outside of the doors, and the televisions are not flat screen.

There are more than 30 themed suites—Gone with the Wind, Fifties, Camelot, Big Apple, 20 Thousand Leagues, Captain's Quarters, and more—plus whirlpool, presidential, and executive suites. Two indoor pools and hot tubs stay open past midnight. A game room is also on site. A hot buffet breakfast is served as late as 10 a.m.; a local entertainer performs during breakfast. ($$)

GRETNA ROAD

Gretna Road offers a quick (for Branson) way to get just about anywhere. It's home to the White House Theatre, the Shoppes at Branson Meadows, and Branson Mall Craft Village.

THE CABINS AT GRAND MOUNTAIN
(245 S Wildwood Dr. ☎ 800.864.4145

❂ branson-missouri-cabins.com) These luxurious but rustic-style cabins sit just off the Strip behind the Grand Plaza Hotel, a perfect choice for those wanting to be in the heart of Branson but still feel as if they're in the great outdoors. The cabins are close to shopping, shows, and Thousand Hills golf resort, which runs the property.

Two-, three-, and four-bedroom cabins are available, sleeping up to 16. They have full-sized and fully stocked kitchens, washers and dryers, gas fireplaces, hardwood flooring, and screened back porches with ceiling fans and hot tubs. Rates vary depending on the season; check the website for specials.

Lodging

The layout and location of these cabins make them a fairly economical and suitable choice for multiple families traveling together.

COMFORT INN & SUITES

(5150 Gretna Rd. ☎ 417.335.4731 🖲 comfortinn.com) This hotel is comfortable and well located, and it has the rustic feel many people look for when coming to Branson. It is near Sight and Sound Theaters and the Yakov Smirnoff Theatre.

The room price includes a hot breakfast and free high-speed Internet. Rooms are equipped with microwave, refrigerator, and coffeemaker. Newspapers are delivered to rooms Monday through Friday. Facilities include a beautiful indoor pool, a hot tub, and a sauna as well as a small fitness center. ($$)

WELK RESORT

(91984 Highway 165 ☎ 417.336.3575 🖲 welkbranson.com) Location is just one of many things attracting people to the Welk Resort year after year. A recent remodeling of its 158 rooms provides even better features, including brand new beds. All guests will appreciate refrigerators, coffee makers and flat screen televisions. (A microwave is available in the lobby.) Timeshare condos are also onsite and occasionally available to rent.

Parents can hardly park the car before kids are running to the splashatorium with its giant waterslide, indoor/outdoor pool, and water play area. The splashatorium is open only to resort guests and admission is included in the price of the room. Anyone not interested in the waterpark can request a discount off their room price. Kids also enjoy a playground and mini golf on the back side of the property. An activities center and extremely knowledgeable concierge can assist with show tickets, reservations and other recreation ideas.

A 2,300 seat theater is also on the Welk Resort property. Big names like Mel Tillis, Chuck Berry, Alabama and even Lynyrd Skynyrd have played here. Tony Orlando is a regular during the Christmas season performing for about eight weeks in November and December.

The Stage Door Canteen serves a breakfast and dinner buffet on site. The dining room is clean but definitely not fancy. Lunch is from the menu during the warmer months and buffet-style during fall and winter. They serve mainly comfort foods like pot roast, meat loaf, pot pies, chicken and ham and more. The soups are made from scratch and you can taste the difference. ($-$$)

INDIAN POINT/SILVER DOLLAR CITY

Situated between town and Branson West, this is a more rural area, with lots of camping and resorts. Silver Dollar City and Indian Point are the main attractions. Highway 265 offers a straight shot to Table Rock Lake.

BEST WESTERN BRANSON INN AT SILVER DOLLAR CITY

(8514 Hwy 76 ☎ 417.338.2141 ❂ bestwesternbransoninn.com)
Those heading to Silver Dollar City will especially appreciate this 145-room hotel's free hot breakfast and complimentary shuttle to and from the park. Rooms are uncluttered and comfortable and feature private balconies. Microwaves and

Lodging

refrigerators can be rented. Jacuzzi suites are available. Along with a huge indoor pool, parents of toddlers will appreciate the kiddie pool. Other facilities include a hot tub and a game room. Barbecue grills are available for guest use. ($$)

LODGES AT TABLE ROCK
(16 Willow Oak Ln. ☎ 800.313.8530 🖱 grandcrowneresorts.com)
These luxury cabins are for larger groups—a good choice for families joining together for a Silver Dollar City vacation. Accommodations range from four to six bedrooms. All the cabins have a spacious and comfortable yet rustic ambiance, and all bedrooms are master suites with jetted tubs. Each cabin has a full kitchen with dishwasher, a sleeper sofa, a fireplace, a vaulted ceiling and hardwood flooring, and a washer/dryer. For the warmer months, there's a furnished screened-in porch. Pets are welcome in designated lodges.

There are indoor and outdoor pools, a fitness center, and a clubhouse pavilion. Other amenities include an activities room with various things going on for the kids; courts for basketball, volleyball, badminton, and tennis; a nice playground; and a small game room. ($$$)

STILL WATERS RESORT
(21 Stillwater Trail ☎ 417.338.2323 🖱 stillwatersresort.com)
Located near Silver Dollar City, Still Waters Resort is truly a favorite among Branson regulars. Families are especially drawn here thanks to the many kid-friendly (and budget-friendly) amenities.

This is a large resort with a wide variety of newly renovated motel rooms and condos to accommodate any size group. All motel rooms have microwaves, mini-refrigerators, and coffee makers. Studios come with kitchenettes and private balconies and lakeview studios have two-person whirlpool tubs. Condos are available with one to four bedrooms. They feature larger kitchens, separate bedrooms and even washers and dryers. Some even have fireplaces. A private lake house is the ultimate in luxury and privacy offering seclusion as well as convenience. There is no daily maid service here but towels can be exchanged at a couple of different sites.

There are plenty of fun freebies at this resort. Paddleboats, kayaks, bikes, inner tubes and cane poles are all free of charge to guests. There are three pools on site. One has a huge water-slide dubbed "the flume." The Island Oasis has the feel of a tropical vacation with its rock surfaces and cascading waterfall. Swim under a bridge to a smaller beach-entry area which is shallow enough for little ones to play. There are also three hot tubs and two kiddie pools. Near the waterslide is a game room and in the center of the resort guests can enjoy horseshoes, basketball, sand volleyball and a playground. Every building is also equipped with a barbeque.

A marina is available for guests wishing to rent wave runners, ski boats or pontoons. Of course, docks are also available for those bringing their own boat. A marketplace is on property to stock up on essentials or souvenirs. There is also a concierge to help with show tickets, dinner reservations or any general information about the area. ($-$$$)

STONEBRIDGE RESORT
(50 Stonebridge Pkwy, Branson West ☎ 866.322.1373
⊎ stonebridgebranson.com) An entire community near Silver

Dollar City and Table Rock Lake, StoneBridge Resort features comfortable cabins, restaurants, walking trails, a private catch-and-release lake, playgrounds, tennis, volleyball, basketball, swimming, a fitness center, and golf.

This resort has the feel of a large and well-kept neighborhood. Roads with names like Fox Hollow and Roark Creek wind through the scenic property past water features and a private lake. The cabins are rustic in decor, with hardwood floors, fireplaces, fully stocked kitchens, and separate bedrooms. Bathrooms feature jetted tubs and separate showers. The only downside is the check-out time, earlier than some at 10 a.m. ($$-$$$)

THE TRIBESMAN RESORT

(416 Cave Ln. ☎ 800.447.3327 ☷ tribesmanresort.com) Located at Indian Point on Table Rock Lake, this is a good choice for families looking for a lake house to call home while on vacation. These are casual one- to five-bedroom cottage and apartment-style accommodations with kitchens and large dining room tables. Furnishings are not fancy, but they are comfortable. For swimmers not looking to share water with the fish, there are five pools and three hot tubs.

The Tribesman is family run and family oriented, with a toddler toy room, a hook-and-line service where kids are taught how to fish, and a coffee spot near the office for parents to unwind. (They'll teach the adults to fish, too, if necessary.) There are special activities nearly every day. These might include a fishing tournament for the kids, a scavenger hunt, a hot dog picnic day, or a free ice cream social. There are about 2 miles of nature trails on the property; stop by the office to pick up a map and find out how kids can become official Trail Rangers. Guests can bring their own boats or rent them at the resort marina. ($$-$$$)

THE VILLAGE AT INDIAN POINT

(24 Village Trail ☎ 417.338.8800 ⬤ thevillageatindianpoint.com)

These beautiful cabin-like condos have modern amenities with a rustic lodge decor. Each unit features a full kitchen, a fireplace, and a separate living area. Options include a lakefront view, a loft condo with spiral staircase, and Jacuzzi tubs. Six to eight people can fit comfortably in a condo.

Outdoor activities include a pool, children's playground, basketball, tetherball, a fishing dock (free children's poles are available), walking paths, and barbecue areas. Indoors, guests have the use of a fitness center, spa and indoor pool. Meeting and banquet rooms are available for group events. Pets are welcome in select units for an additional fee. ($$-$$$)

THE WILDERNESS LOG CABINS AND CAMPGROUND

(5125 Hwy 265 ☎ 800.477.5164 ⬤ thewildernesslogcabins.com)

This facility is located near Silver Dollar City, and a shuttle leaves every couple of hours for the attraction. Several types of cabins are available. The least expensive is the Pioneer. That's exactly the kind of experience it offers (no bathroom), but with a queen bed and a set of bunk beds. Cabins have heating and air conditioning, a table with chairs, and a ceiling fan. Outside are a fire ring and a water spigot. Three nearby bathrooms are newly renovated, with private showers.

Rustic cabins have the amenities of the Pioneer cabins plus a bathroom and shower, a microwave, cable TV, a coffeepot, a small refrigerator, and a gas grill. There are a couple of rocking chairs on the deck. Rustic cabins with kitchenettes and fireplaces are available for an added cost. Loft cabins have the same amenities, with a queen bed, two full beds, and a twin. Loft options include a kitchenette and fireplace, and a jetted tub.

The Wilderness has three playgrounds and a swimming pool. A nicely equipped game room offers video games, pool tables, high-speed Internet, and cable television. Most of the 39 cabins require a two-day minimum stay, three days on holiday weekends. No pets are allowed other than service animals. ($-$$$)

TABLE ROCK LAKE/HWY 165

This is a little out of the way from the lights of Branson and appeals to those looking for waterfront peace and quiet. The Table Rock Lake/Highway 165 area is home to State Park Marina, the Showboat Branson Belle, Dewey Short Visitors Center, Table Rock Dam and overlook, Shepherd of the Hills Fish Hatchery, and Moonshine Beach.

CHATEAU ON THE LAKE
(415 N. Hwy 265 ☎ 417.334.1161

☏ **chateauonthelakebranson.com)** This stunning European-style hotel looks like a castle sitting on a cliff overlooking the waters of Table Rock Lake. The impression continues after stepping inside the ten-story sky-lit atrium lobby. Nature is all around: there are trees and fresh flowers, a waterfall, and even a stream with a koi pond in this beautiful entry area.

Quality touches include leather seating, plush mattresses, feather pillows, and down comforters. All of the 301 rooms have 32-inch flat screen televisions, coffeemakers, and in-room safes. Vanities are separate from the bathrooms. Accommodations range from standard to lakefront and presidential suites.

Amenities include a marina with boats, jet skis, and snorkeling and scuba equipment. Scuba lessons are available. The Crawdaddies Kids Club entertains children between four and 12 with games, crafts, and special activities; reservations are required. The Chateau also offers an outdoor playground, lighted tennis courts (with complimentary balls and rackets), and both indoor and outdoor pools.

The Spa Chateau is probably one of the most pampering experiences in Branson. The 14,000-square-foot facility, connected to the Chateau by an indoor walkway, offers European therapies and a surreal Roman bath underneath a waterfall, with views onto Table Rock Lake. A yoga movement studio also offers lake views. Treatments include massages, facials, and a barber spa for men. An "image center" provides manicures and pedicures, paraffin treatments, and hair services. A steam room and sauna are part of the spa.

This is an expensive resort, so it's appreciated when there are no extra charges for many services. High-speed Internet is free. Also free is unlimited access to canoes and paddleboats, as is the panoramic telescope viewing from the patio. Another enjoyable freebie is the small Sassafras Movie Theatre in the lower level, complete with complimentary popcorn.

Lodging

Several types of dining options are offered at the Chateau. The deli offers salads, sandwiches, pizza, and to-go picnic meals. Relax near the indoor waterfall at the Atrium Café which serves a casual breakfast, lunch, and dinner as well as late evening cocktails. The Sweet Shoppe offers decadent candies, cakes and ice cream creations. Finally, the Chateau Grille is an elegant fine dining experience.

The Chateau offers a number of special packages throughout the year, and active military personnel receive a 20 percent discount. Holidays are special here, with fireworks displays on Memorial Day, 4th of July, Labor Day and New Year's Eve. Christmas lights and decorations are magnificent and elves are available to tuck in the kids for a magical experience. This is a *AAA Four Diamond* Resort. ($$$)

THE MAJESTIC AT TABLE ROCK LAKE
(245 S Wildwood Dr. ☎ 800.495.4653
🖱 majestic-at-table-rock.com) The name is entirely appropriate for these waterfront condominiums created and operated by Thousand Hills Golf Resort. The furnishings, view, and amenities make for a majestic stay.

The Majestic is just a couple of miles from Table Rock Dam and is close to the Branson Belle. Condos with two, three, or four bedrooms feature large and fully stocked kitchens with granite countertops, the latest appliances, and both an indoor eating area and a screened dining room. The beds are luxurious and comfortable. A pool is on site for the warmer months.

Lodging

The Majestic feels more like a home than a hotel. It is a nice option for longer stays or a multifamily group. Be aware that checkout time is firm at 11 a.m. ($$-$$$)

WESTGATE EMERALD POINTE

(750 Emerald Pointe Dr., Hollister ☎ 888.808.7410

🖱 wgemeraldpointe.com) Westgate Emerald Pointe has one- and two-bedroom suites with views of Table Rock Lake. Even the basic suite is spacious and comfortable, with a fully equipped kitchen, washer/dryer, sleeper sofa, and DVD player. Deluxe suites include whirlpool tubs and balconies.

Among other amenities are a 9-hole miniature golf course, indoor and outdoor pools, a hot tub, a basketball court, an exercise facility, and barbecue grills. Pets are welcome with a paid deposit, but there are breed limitations; call for details. ($-$$$)

LAKE TANEYCOMO

This is where the trout fishermen want to be! Taneycomo is too cold for swimming, but regardless of whether or not you fish, this is a nice area in which to experience Ozarks scenery and still be just a short drive from the action.

BLUFF HOUSE

(806 Acacia Club Rd ☎ 866.522.3276

🖱 bransonluxurylodging.com) Built by Bass Pro Founder, Johnny Morris, the Bluff House is the place to go when you're ready to splurge on rustic luxury. Among many highlights are the floor to ceiling windows which offer a stunning view of Branson.

Lodging

Eagles live in nearby trees and, while only sometimes seen, they can often be heard.

The cabin, near Lake Taneycomo, is situated high in a wooded, private setting. The 2,500 square foot log home has two bedrooms and a loft, three baths and three fireplaces. It also features a waterfall shower which was built into the side of a rock bluff. There is also a wine cellar, three fireplaces and a plunge pool.

The Bluff House is ideal for romantic getaways or family vacations. Its location offers seclusion yet is close enough to enjoy all Branson has to offer.

LILLEY'S LANDING RESORT AND MARINA

(367 River Ln ☎ 417.334.6380 ▮ lilleyslanding.com) Just steps from Lake Taneycomo, Lilley's Landing is ideal for fishermen and their families. It's a small, family-run resort that feels like home, with a generous playground and a pool for the kids. There are 24 kitchenette units ranging in size from one to four bedrooms. Prices are more than reasonable. Located just 2 miles from the Strip, this is a convenient choice for show-goers who also want to enjoy the Ozark surroundings. Even for those not looking for a place to stay, the Lilley's marina has plenty of equipment for fishing on Lake Taneycomo. ($$)

SHEPHERD OF THE HILLS

This central Branson location is home to the Pierce Arrow, Shoji, Little Opry, Hamner Barber, IMAX, and Kirby VanBurch theaters. There are a number of restaurants, including chains like Red Lobster and Olive Garden. McFarlain's inside the IMAX is a nice choice, or check out the largest Golden Corral in the nation.

BARRINGTON HOTEL & SUITES

(263 Shepherd of the Hills Expy ☎ 800.760.8866

☻ barringtonhotel.com) Newly renovated with hardwood floors and a stone fireplace, the Barrington also shows an attention to detail in guest rooms, with comfortable beds and nice furnishings. An indoor pool, hot tub, and fitness center are available to guests. This is a pet-friendly hotel for animals 20 pounds and under.

A refrigerator, a coffeemaker, Internet access, and flat screen television are provided in each of the 145 rooms. Jacuzzi, honeymoon, and presidential suites are available. A free continental breakfast served every morning includes waffles, pastries, biscuits and gravy, and more. ($$)

HONEYSUCKLE INN & CONFERENCE CENTER

(3598 Shepherd of the Hills Expy ☎ 417.335.2030

☻ honeysuckleinn.com) This welcoming and beautifully landscaped property is in a prime location next to RFD-TV The Theater and the IMAX complex at Highway 76 and Shepherd of the Hills Expressway. Rooms are fairly spacious and comfortable.

Starting off with what comes free of charge at the Honeysuckle Inn: coffee and cookies are available in the lobby 24/7, there's complimentary breakfast every morning, high-speed Internet is free, and kids 11 and under stay free. Amenities include an enormous outdoor pool, a warm indoor pool, and a six-person hot tub. Each of the 210 rooms is equipped with hair dryer, ironing board, and flat screen TV. The Honeysuckle has meeting rooms for large and small groups. Catering is available for any type of gathering. ($)

WESTGATE BRANSON WOODS

(2201 Roark Valley Dr. ☎ 877.253.8572 🖱 wgbransonwoods.com)
Branson Woods has accommodations for a range of budgets, from hotel rooms to condos and cabins. All guests receive access to the resort's amenities and activities.

Hotel rooms are pretty basic but do include a microwave, a mini-refrigerator, and a coffeemaker; both king and queen rooms are offered. Condo suites range from studios to four-bedroom units. The studio suites aren't much bigger than the hotel rooms but feel a little more upscale. Larger suites include full kitchen, fireplace, patio, whirlpool tub, and sleeper sofa.

Westgate cabins offer privacy with rustic luxury. They have the feel of a cabin, but there's no roughing it, thanks to the amenities. The smallest cabin, a one-bedroom, is just over 500 square feet and can accommodate four. The largest, a four-bedroom, is 2,300 square feet and can sleep up to ten.

Westgate Pizza Company is on the property, offering a convenient meal option. Activities at the resort include basketball, volleyball, ping pong, playgrounds, bike rentals, hiking trails, campfire and barbecue areas, and even shuffleboard. There are indoor and outdoor swimming pools. This is a pet-friendly hotel, with certain guidelines; call for specifics. ($-$$$)

Lodging

SURROUNDING AREA

Just a short drive from Branson are small towns and big resorts. Hollister is home to the College of the Ozarks' Mabee Lodge, and Ye Olde English Inn is situated in the town's quaint historic district. Big Cedar Lodge is worth the short drive to visit.

BIG CEDAR LODGE ✪ Must See!
(612 Devil's Pool Rd., Ridgedale ☎ 417.339.5200
🖰 big-cedar.com) "America's Premier Wilderness Resort" is a five-star experience, an ideal spot for a honeymoon, family reunion, or other special occasion. Just a short drive south of Branson on Highway 65, Big Cedar Lodge is hidden in the Ozark landscape with tremendous views of Table Rock Lake. Free shuttles run 24 hours a day to transport guests anywhere on the property as well as to nearby Dogwood Canyon.

Lodging is offered for a range of budgets: private cabins, cottages, and three different lodges. All have an upscale rustic feel, and a 2,500-square-foot governor's suite is the ultimate in luxury. Active military are honored with a ten percent discount and a framed photo of fireworks over the lake.

Many of the cabins are themed; there are NASCAR cabins, a Ducks Unlimited cabin, even a Kevin Costner cabin. All feature a wood-burning fireplace, a full kitchen, flat screen television, and lake views; many have Jacuzzi tubs. Complimentary snack baskets and beverages, cookies delivered to the room each night, and wood stacked on the porch come without asking. Full-size grills are available on the deck. Knotty Pine Cabins at Thunderhead Point, smaller but close to the lake, are geared to fishermen. The three lodges are economical options that offer spacious rooms, some with fireplace, kitchenette, and Jacuzzi.

Recreation possibilities include the 9-hole Top of the Rock Golf Course, tennis, shuffleboard, miniature golf, a shooting "school," and even scuba diving. During peak seasons there are family games, bonfires, ice cream socials, and "dive in" movies at the pool. Wagon rides, romantic carriage rides, and trail rides are all available. The wagon rides end with a bonfire and s'mores, or groups can ride to a special chuckwagon dinner, sometimes accompanied by "Singing Cowboy" Clay Self.

Complimentary activities for kids from four to 12 may include dive-in movies (at the pool), fishing, and a welcoming bonfire. For-fee sessions at Little Cedar Kids' Club include three hours of environmental awareness–themed games, art, and snacks. Special themed days occur from Memorial Day through Labor Day.

Two spas are staffed by trained estheticians and therapists. A photography studio is on site to capture a family vacation picture. Tell the front desk staff if you're celebrating a special occasion, and cake and a balloon will be delivered to your room—or, for kids, a "cookie monster" treat. ($$$)

Bent Hook Marina. This marina is solely for the use of Big Cedar guests. Fishermen are likely to be inspired just by stepping into the market and seeing the fish swimming under a cut-out in the floor. Complimentary paddleboats are available, and there are Tracker boats to rent. A ski school offers instruction on how to slalom, kneeboard, and wakeboard.

Christmas at Big Cedar. Each public area is adorned with a fantastical Christmas tree. Even the private cabins have fully decorated trees. The entire grounds are lit up, and the display of lights can be enjoyed on an evening wagon ride around the property. There are special holiday productions, special surprises during the 12 days before Christmas, even baking with Mrs. Santa. A memorable experience for children is the Elf Tuck-in; for a fee, an elf comes to your room and spends some time with the kids before tucking them in. ($$$)

GOOD CENTER ACCOMODATIONS
(1 Opportunity Ave., Point Lookout ☎ 417.239.1900
keetercenter.edu) Good Center is located just behind the College of the Ozark's Keeter Center, a few minutes' drive south of Branson. These rooms, similar to traditional hotel rooms but continuing Keeter Center's rustic decor theme, are comfortable and clean, staffed by students at the college. They are also a little easier on the wallet than the college's Mabee Lodge suites. Choices include a hillside view or, for a few more dollars, a lakeside view. All rooms include television, iron and ironing board, and feather pillows. ($$)

MABEE LODGE ★ Must See!
(1 Opportunity Ave., Point Lookout ☎ 417.239.1900
keetercenter.edu) What an experience to stay at the College of the Ozarks' Mabee Lodge! Gigantic fireplaces and comfortable leather seating adorn the lobby. A glass elevator takes guests to the 30 rooms and suites located inside the Keeter Center, a perfect combination of first-class resort and rustic cabin.

Lodging

Fireplaces, leather furniture, patios, jetted tubs, and kitchenettes are just the beginning. Turndown service includes robes and mints, homemade cookies, and milk from the college dairy. The beds are luxurious. Guests wake up to a hot breakfast served in their rooms, included in the room rate. Staffed by students from the College of the Ozarks working to pay for their tuition, Mabee Lodge is light years away from dorm life. ($$$)

PORT OF KIMBERLING RESORT

(49 Lake Rd., Kimberling City ☎ 417.739.2315 ⬧ mypok.com)
This newest addition to the popular Port of Kimberling is clean, comfortable, and has beautiful views of Table Rock Lake. It's a nice choice for people looking for a lake vacation minus the tent and cook stove.

All 39 rooms have microwaves and compact refrigerators and plenty of storage. Suites have full kitchens and the extra space is often worth the splurge. Connecting rooms can be requested for larger groups. Ask for a lake view room to take advantage of the scenery.

The heated outdoor pool is unique with a beach-style entry and shooting jets of water; it's a perfect area for little ones to splash and play. The pool is just off the hotel's meeting room making it ideal for birthday parties or family reunions. Other amenities include a fitness center with weights and cardio equipment, business center and snacks available for purchase near the front desk.

In addition to its hotel rooms, Port of Kimberling has a full service marina and campground with cabins, RV hookups and

Lodging

tent camping available. Be sure to ask about special offers. This resort has been a family-owned property for four generations. It shows in the service and attention to detail. ($$)

YE OLDE ENGLISH INN
(24 Downing St., Hollister ☎ 417.544.9056

☗ oldenglishinnhollister.com) Fans of romance author Janet Dailey will be interested to know she is the owner of Ye Old English Inn. The Elizabethan-style architectural details and intimate feel make this a fitting choice for a romance author or anyone looking to transform a Branson vacation into a retreat. Built in 1909, the inn is listed on the National Register of Historic Places. There are rumors that President Truman, Cary Grant, and even Clark Gable stayed here. Curved railings, the original terrazzo floors, and three-dimensional artwork are among the appealing features. The inn is often used as a wedding venue.

There are 21 guest rooms, some connecting; three are some-what larger deluxe rooms, and two are suites with sitting areas. All feature queen beds. Sleeping quarters are very small, but public spaces are comfortable and make a good setting for family gatherings or meeting other guests. There are no ground-floor rooms, nor is there an elevator. Breakfast is avail-able next door at the River Stone Restaurant. On the other side of the inn is The Black Horse Pub.

Lodging

THE STRIP/HIGHWAY 76

This is where the majority of shows, restaurants, lodging, and traffic are found. For those wanting to be in the middle of it all, this is where to stay.

CLARION HOTEL AT THE PALACE ✪ Must See!

(2820 W. Hwy 76 ☎ 417.334.7666 🖱 clarionhotel.com) This hotel boasts numerous awards and the distinction of hosting President George Bush Sr. and Mrs. Bush. It has everything, including a great location. It's right in the middle of the Strip, making it possible to walk to many shows and restaurants. The rooms are spacious and the beds comfortable. Amenities include mini-refrigerators, microwaves, and coffeemakers. Most rooms have small private balconies. A laundry facility is on site.

This is a large property with a total of 166 rooms in two separate towers. The hotel has a fitness center, pool, sauna, and hot tub indoors. Outside there is another hot tub and a pool with a water feature in the center. Buckingham's restaurant is in the Clarion.

The Clarion offers plenty of complimentary extras, including continental breakfast, high-speed Internet, weekday newspaper, local calls, and coffee in the lobby. Shuttle service to and from Branson or Springfield airport is available for a fee. This is a beautiful hotel anytime, but holiday travelers will appreciate its lovely seasonal decorations. ($$)

DUTTON FAMILY INN

(3454 W. Hwy 76 ☎ 417.334.8873 🖱 duttoninn.com) The Dutton Family Inn sits just behind the family's popular theater.

Newly renovated, it is a recommended choice for those looking for economy lodging. The memory foam mattresses and pillows alone make this a comfortable place to stay. In fact, the pillows are so popular that guests can actually buy their own at Abby's Tourist Trap next to the theater.

Other amenities include free Wi-Fi, coffeemaker, hair dryer, guest laundry, and hot breakfast. There is no pool, but Dutton Inn guests are allowed to use the pool and hot tub at the Super 8 hotel next door—just tell the front desk when you are heading over for a swim. There's no charge for children 12 and under. ($)

GRAND COUNTRY WATERPARK RESORT

(1945 W Hwy 76 ☎ 417.335.3535 📱 grandcountry.com) A full Branson experience can be had at Grand Country without ever leaving the parking lot. Shows, food, games, an indoor water-park, and the hotel are all here within walking distance. The resort location on the west end of the Strip means it's just a short drive to many shows, including the Dixie Stampede.

Accommodations are clean but beginning to show their age. Rooms offer basic necessities (including a coffeemaker). What some might find lacking is quickly forgotten when they take advantage of free admission to the indoor-outdoor Splash Country Waterpark.

Breakfast is not included in the room rate but is available at the Grand Country Buffet, and well worth the price. Other dining options include The Mining Company Grill, Glenn's Frozen Custard, and Papa Grand's Pizza (home of the world's largest banjo). Pizza can also be delivered to guest rooms.

Lodging

The Fun Spot is the place for black-light miniature golf, mini-bowling, a laser maze, and an arcade. There is a play area where kids can simply run around and be kids. Grand Country also has its own theater, featuring such shows as Comedy Jamboree and Amazing Pets. ($$)

GRAND PLAZA HOTEL

(245 N Wildwood Dr. ☎ 417.336.6646

☗ **bransongrandplaza.com)** This large and beautiful hotel makes an imposing impression from its spot just off Highway 76. Inside, the lobby has a spacious and comfortable look, with leather couches and wingback chairs. Besides queen and king rooms, there are mini-suites, honeymoon suites, and family units. Larger rooms have two-person whirlpool tubs, mini-refrigerators, and microwaves. There is free Internet access in all rooms, and a computer terminal is available in the lobby 24 hours a day.

The hotel has an indoor pool, hot tub, fitness center, and game room. It features a complimentary hot breakfast every morning. The Plaza View Restaurant and Lounge is also open for a casual lunch or dinner; parents will appreciate the kids' menu. The lobby gift shop also serves as a concierge, arranging tickets, reservations, and transportation. ($$)

LODGE OF THE OZARKS

(3431 W Hwy 76 ☎ 417.334.7535 ☗ lodgeoftheozarks.com) This impressive hotel sits right in the middle of the Strip next to the Hughes Brothers Theater. Conveniently located near Gretna Road, it offers easy access to many shows. The rooms are spacious, with updated furnishings and fixtures including flat screen televisions.

There are several types of rooms, some with large Jacuzzi tubs. Nice extras include generously sized toiletries along with vanity and sewing kits. Robes are also provided. There are coffee-makers in every room. Cribs and rollaway beds cost extra, as does breakfast in the adjoining restaurant. There is a small fitness room on site as well as an immaculate pool and a hot tub. With its nearly floor-to-ceiling windows, the pool area is a peaceful oasis in the midst of the Branson bustle. ($$)

SAVANNAH HOUSE

(165 Expressway Ln ☎ 417.336.3132

✆ savannahhousebranson.com) The Savannah House looks just as expected, given its name: a southern beauty with large columns gracing the front porch. Outdoor rocking chairs and tables overlook beautiful landscaping that includes a waterfall and a gazebo.

One of the unique things about this hotel is the checkout time: late-risers will love the luxury of a 1 p.m. deadline. Another nice perk is a late-night dessert of fruit cobbler, ice cream, or cookies. A hot breakfast is also included in the room price.

Regular rooms are basic but clean and comfortable. Other options include king Jacuzzi suites and two-bedroom presidential suites. An outdoor pool and fitness center are among hotel amenities. The staff is friendly and always ready to help. For anyone planning to see shows at the Mansion or anywhere along Shepherd of the Hills Expressway, this location is convenient. ($$)

Lodging

The Branson area has beautiful hiking trails, both paved and natural terrain.

Restaurants

There is no lack of restaurants in Branson. Every type of cuisine in virtually every kind of atmosphere is available. Having trouble coming to a consensus? Try one of the many buffet restaurants; the local Golden Corral is the nation's largest and definitely has something for everyone. Those looking for fine dining should consider Level 2 Steakhouse. Wonderful pastries are found at Dino's 24-Karrot Café. If simply having pizza delivered to the room sounds appealing, look no further than Pizza World.

Prices are compared with other restaurants within each section. $=less expensive; $$=more expensive; $$$=most expensive.

COFFEE/TEA HOUSES

For lunch or just a great latte, Branson's coffee houses offer appealing variety and atmosphere.

DINO'S 24KARROT CAKE COMPANY ⭐ Must See!

(307 Branson Landing Rd ☎ 417.334.0223) Piano showman Dino Kartsonakis has known fame for decades as a performer and television personality in the Christian entertainment world. Now Dino is going back to his boyhood roots and unleashing a passion for cooking learned from his chef parents.

The 24-Karrot is enjoyable anytime, but when Dino is in town it's truly an experience. He's sure to ask if everyone's happy, and he may even pull up a chair and join guests in a meal.

The food is fresh and satisfying. Choices include soups, sandwiches, and pizza; the chicken salad on pretzel bread is excellent. Do not leave without dessert. Even if you don't like carrot cake, try this one—incredibly moist, with just the right blend of spices, no raisins, and plenty of frosting. Dino's cakes are sold at many restaurants around town and are available online. ($-$$)

THE GARDENS RESTAURANT

(4580 Gretna Rd. ☎ 417.334.9598 🖥 thegardensrestaurant.com) With its warm decor and plentiful greenery, this restaurant in the Branson Meadows shopping center offers a lovely and relaxing ambiance. The food is excellent, and there's a nice variety. The spiced walnut salad is recommended. In addition there are soups, sandwiches, vegetarian selections, and daily specials. A heartier menu is offered for dinner, when there is sometimes live entertainment. ($-$$$)

STARBUCKS

(201 E Main St. ☎ 417.334.1390 🖥 starbucks.com) For those used to having a Starbucks drive-thru on every corner, Branson may be a bit of a shock. There is only one drive-thru location in town. It is located downtown near the Branson Landing. There is a also a Starbucks located inside of Branson's **Target** *(☎ 417.243.4500)* located near Highway 65 and Branson Hills Parkway.

SUGAR LEAF TREATS ✪ Must See!

(Grand Village, 2800 W. Hwy 76, Ste. 211 ☎ 417.336.6618 🖥 sugarleaftreats.com) Sugar Leaf Treats is an oasis in the midst of the craziness of the Strip. Located in the Grand Village shopping center, this enchanting teahouse serves decadent quiche, muffins, and breakfast sandwiches. Everything, from breads to sauces, is homemade. Lunch is worth the wait, especially for the ultimate BLT with pepperjack and turkey. A Cajun turkey wrap is another favorite.

Diners will definitely want to leave room for dessert; the coconut cream pie is a specialty. When it's chilly outside, stop in for a comforting hot chocolate topped with a giant homemade marshmallow. Sugar Leaf also does catering and makes custom cakes and cupcakes. It is highly recommended.($-$$)

DESSERTS

When the sweet tooth needs to be satisfied there are plenty of decadent choices in Branson. From the old fashioned ice cream parlor downtown to the extravagant cakes at Dino's 24-Karrot Cake Café, it is easy to find an excuse to indulge.

ANDY'S FROZEN CUSTARD ✪ Must See!

(3415 W Hwy 76 ☎ 417.337.5501 ✆ eatandys.com) Forget the diet. Forget the budget. This is absolutely worth the splurge. There may be other frozen custard places, but none like Andy's. It's like taking ice cream to the most decadent level possible and then throwing candy on top. Concretes are a favorite; pick your favorite toppings, and they'll be mixed into the custard. For sundae lovers, the Ozarks Turtle is a good choice. A couple of important warnings: the James Brownie Funky Jackhammer should only be attempted by serious chocolate–peanut butter lovers. Also, it might be best to wait until the end of a vacation to visit Andy's, or it might become a habit-forming budget (and belt) breaker. ($$)

MR. B'S ICE CREAM PARLOR & DELI

(102 S Business 65 ☎ 417.336.5735) Mr. B's is a small, old-fashioned ice cream parlor with black-and-white checkered floors and Coca-Cola memorabilia. There are tons of choices here, including 20 flavors of ice cream, sundaes, shakes, and old-fashioned sodas. Mr. B's also offers lunch items, including nachos, hot dogs, steakburgers, and chicken or tuna salad on honey wheat bread. This is a cute place to stop for a bite to eat or some dessert. ($-$$)

SMACK'S DELI AND ICE CREAM

(104 W Main St. ☎ 417.336.2731) Hungry shoppers can find a quick and satisfying bite to eat at Smack's Deli and Ice Cream, a small restaurant across the street from Dick's 5 & 10. The atmosphere is casual; diners order at the counter. Sandwiches are served on homemade sweet bread. The homemade chicken salad is a specialty, as is the Reuben. Nathan's quarter-pound hot dogs are also on the menu.

Smack's serves Blue Bell ice cream in 16 flavors. The waffle cones are homemade from a special recipe. Shakes, malts, cobblers, and apple dumplings with ice cream and apple cinnamon sauce round out the dessert offerings. ($)

BARBECUE

This may not be Kansas City but there is still some great barbeque in town. Danna's and Famous Dave's are highly recommended when the barbeque craving hits.

DANNA'S BARBEQUE ⭐ Must See!

(963 Hwy 165 ☎ 417.337.5527 🖰 dannasbbq.com) This is some
of the best barbecue around. The pulled pork is memorable,
especially when it's served on garlic toast. (Just ask for it.) The
fries are outstanding. Danna's is also known for its burgers,
catfish, ribs, and smoked chicken. A favorite for the hungriest
patrons is the Big, Big Pig, a pulled pork sandwich with twice
the meat as normal and even some sausage on top. For dessert,
Danna's serves dollar sundaes or more serious sweets like
Bananas Foster and homemade brownies with frozen custard.
($$)

FAMOUS DAVES

(1201 Branson Landing Blvd. ☎ 417.334.4858
🖰 **famousdaves.com)** Many are already familiar with this popular
barbeque chain. This restaurant, located on Branson Landing,
will not disappoint. It's a casual atmosphere for families to
get their fingers dirty on ribs, wings, and chicken. Burgers and
barbeque sandwiches are just as good and, if there's room, the
desserts are worth the splurge. ($$)

BUFFETS

Buffets are an easy and economical way to please a variety of
palates. Among its popular buffet restaurants Branson is home
to the world's largest Golden Corral restaurant.

GOLDEN CORRAL ⭐ Must See!

(3551 Shepherd of the Hills Expy ☎ 417.336.6297
🖰 **goldencorralbranson.com)** This is the largest Golden Corral
restaurant in the world. It can feed more than 650 people at

a time, and chances are they're all going to leave happy. The choices are tremendous, with more than 150 lunch and dinner items, fresh and of good quality. The restaurant also serves breakfast.

A buffet highlight is the steak and carved meats station. Steak is cooked to individual preference, the meat seasoned well and the cuts satisfying. Soup, bread, potatoes, pizza, a myriad of vegetables, and even Chinese food are part of this enormous spread. The extensive salad bar can be a meal in itself. For dessert there are cakes, cookies, pies, cobblers, and ice cream with enough toppings to make kids feel their dreams have come true. Those in a hurry can even get their buffet to go. Groups are welcome, and Golden Corral can cater special events.

Golden Corral also has a small theater where singer Barbara Fairchild performs. Performances are included with the buffet price; in fact, diners attending the show get a free beverage their meals. ($$)

GRAND COUNTRY BUFFET

(1945 W Hwy 76 ☎ 417.335.2434 ⬤ grandcountry.com) This restaurant sits in the center of Grand Country Resort, in the same building as the shops and shows. But the buffet is good enough to stand on its own. The breakfast selection is enormous, everything from yogurt and cereal to homemade breads, breakfast meats, and pancakes. The staff is attentive and keeps the buffet well stocked.

Lunch is every bit as good and features a huge variety at the salad bar. Five food bars offer hand-carved meats, vegetables, and just about every kind of dessert one could want. This is not the place for those on a diet, but it is a great place for a filling meal. ($$)

PLANTATION RESTAURANT

(3460 W Hwy 76 ☎ 417.334.7800) This is a highly advertised restaurant, but the food simply doesn't live up to the hype. There is little on the buffet, and what is there looks as if it's been sitting for a while, much of it in visible grease. ($-$$)

CASUAL FARE

These restaurants offer a casual atmosphere while adding to the vacation experience. There are historical diners, floating cafes and places where the bread is thrown across the room.

BILLY GAIL'S CAFE ✪ Must See!

(5291 Hwy 265 ☎ 417.338.8883) Breakfast at Billy Gail's is a favorite tradition for both locals and Branson visitors. This simple log cabin restaurant near Silver Dollar City has all the charm and friendliness of a southern grandma who loves to cook. The atmosphere is definitely country; the building looks older than its 1960s origin would indicate.

Everything at Billy Gail's is made from scratch. Portions are shockingly big. Pancakes are the size of a medium pizza. Omelets are made with four eggs. Those looking for something a little different should try the "sloppy biscuit" with sausage, egg, and cheese smothered in gravy and served with hash browns.

Kids eating at Billy Gail's are presented with a basket of toys, and they get to take one home. Come here often, and Gail will know the kids and their parents on a first-name basis. The register area is cluttered with family photos. The lobby has toys and antiques for sale, and the entire restaurant is filled with "uniqueables," as Gail describes them. The prices are so affordable visitors may come for breakfast and wind up carting away antique canisters.

Breakfast is served all day, from 7 a.m. until 2 p.m. Lunch begins at 11 a.m.; Billy Gail's isn't open for dinner. Things here are done the old-fashioned way—no credit cards, but they accept cash and checks. ($-$$)

BRANSON CAFÉ

(120 W Main St. ☎ 417.334.3021 ✆ thebransoncafe.com) This old-fashioned eatery has been in Branson for more than a hundred years. The decor is cheerful and inviting, with red wood paneling and a red and white striped border. Antiques hanging on the walls give it an old-time feel. The owner does all of the baking, and he definitely has a knack for it. The Branson Café serves a popular breakfast and, for lunch, sandwiches, fried chicken, catfish, and other comfort food. There is also a kids' menu. There are excellent fruit and cream pies for dessert. $

DICK CLARK'S AMERICAN BANDSTAND GRILL

(1600 W. Hwy 76 ☎ 417.332.1960 ✆ dickclarksabbranson.com/abgrill.html) Dick Clark's is casual, fun, and filled with memorabilia. On display are more than 600 items dating as far back as the 1950s, including Ricky Nelson's autographed 12-string acoustic guitar, gold and platinum records, original sheet music, and clothing worn by various stars during performances. Along the walls are pictures from American Bandstand performances. On the ceiling are giant mock 45 LP records.

The menu is also casual, with various salads and a wide variety of sandwiches and burgers. In addition there are fajitas, fish and chips, steak, and comfort foods. Of course, there have to be malts and other fountain items. Beer, wine, and mixed drinks are available from the bar. Drinks have names like Blue Suede Shoes, Proud Mary, and Hey Hey It's a Monkey. ($$)

DOBYN'S DINING

(Keeter Center, College of the Ozarks, 1 Opportunity Ave., Point Lookout ☎ 417.239.1900 🖰 keetercenter.edu) This is a casual dining atmosphere with fine-dining food. Many of the ingredients are grown on the College of the Ozarks campus. Entrées include 21-day aged filet, top sirloin or ribeye steak, pot roast, fish, chicken, meatloaf, and more. Those looking for a lighter meal can find excellent soups and salads. Dobyn's Dining is open daily for lunch and dinner and on Sunday for brunch. Students provide entertainment Thursday through Saturday evenings. ($$-$$$)

FARMHOUSE FAMILY RESTAURANT AND GIFTS

(119 W Main St. ☎ 417.334.9701) Another local favorite, the Farmhouse, has a country decor with wood wainscoting and wallpapered walls hung with a mix of mirrors, small shutters, and other objects. The tables are small and the atmosphere is quaint.

There may be long lines to get into the Farmhouse during busy seasons. Many are waiting for the chicken-fried steak and the cobbler. A gift shop upstairs has a nice selection of frames, baby items, candles, and more. ($-$$)

FLOATING CAFE

(3443 Indian Point Rd. ☎ 417.338.2101 🛑 thefloatingcafe.com)
People have enjoyed eating at the Floating Cafe on Table Rock Lake since the 60s, and not even three tornadoes damaging the small business put a stop to the service. Now customers can enjoy a new facility and two-story deck in the same location on the Indian Point Public Dock. The food is casual: salads, burgers, sandwiches, or typical breakfast fare. A kids' menu is also available. You can eat inside or out on the deck. After feeding yourself, head outside to feed the fish! ($$)

GILLEY'S TEXAS CAFE

(3457 W Hwy 76 ☎ 417.335.2755 🛑 gilleys.com) Country music icon Mickey Gilley takes folks back to his Texas roots with this restaurant next door to his theater. The atmosphere is casual, with tall booths and a Santa Fe–inspired decor. Gilley promises ice-cold beer to go with the fajitas, hamburgers, pork chops, and chicken-fried steak. The menu includes salads, soups, and sandwiches, too. Gilley's also serves frozen margaritas. Gilley's stays open late, so it's a good place to go after the show. Those with a ticket stub from Mickey Gilley's theater receive a ten percent discount. ($$)

LAMBERT'S ✪ Must See!

(1800 W. Hwy J, Ozark ☎ 417.581.7655 🛑 throwedrolls.com)
It's a good idea to fast for several days before making the

40-minute drive north from Branson to Lambert's. The portions served here are huge, the food is memorable, and the atmosphere is nothing but fun. Wooden floors and large wooden booths are surrounded by hanging flags, random metal signs, and pictures.

People love the home-style comfort food, but they really come for the rolls. Be warned: the bread doesn't come in a basket. This is the home of "throwed rolls." People yell for a roll and get it pitched to them, sometimes across the room. Wait for the sorghum to come around and it's carbohydrate heaven. Beyond the rolls and the enormous portions, there are "pass-arounds." Servers wearing suspenders walk around with huge bowls and ladle out macaroni and tomatoes, black-eyed peas, fried potatoes and onions, and fried okra.

Be prepared for a wait, especially on weekends. While waiting, the gift shop has lots of interesting items to see. ($$)

MCFARLAIN'S

(3052 Shepherd of the Hills Expy ☎ 800.419.4832 ☻ bransonimax.com) Located in the IMAX Complex, McFarlain's claims to be "Ozark Cookin' Like It's Spose Ta Be." The restaurant's name comes from the story of the McFarlain family featured in the IMAX film *Ozarks: Legacy & Legend*, which visitors can watch on the big (really big) screen or buy to take home. The sweet cornbread is definitely a star at McFarlain's. The sweet-potato fries are out of this world and made even better by the Hawaiian sauce that comes with them.

Groups of six or more may find themselves seated at the restaurant's "trick" table, which rises ever so slowly while patrons are eating so that eventually they will find themselves raising their arms to reach their food. That's about the time staff will come over and have them stand and sing for the rest of the restaurant. McFarlains is open for breakfast, lunch, and dinner. Go online for discount coupons. ($-$$)

MEL'S HARD LUCK DINER

(2800 W Hwy 76 ☎ 417.332.0150) Situated in the Grand Village shopping center, this place is pure fun. Don't expect a fancy meal—it's a burger-and-fries 50s-style diner. What's unique is the wait staff. All of them are singers, some of whom have made a name for themselves. Jason Yeager and Matt Kester of American Idol fame returned to the Hard Luck Diner even after their success on the show. Everyone gets a front row seat, and the impromptu performances are included with the meal. Lines can be long, though they usually move pretty fast. The food is a little pricey, but people don't seem to mind paying for the Hard Luck experience. ($$)

MOON RIVER GRILL

(2600 W Hwy 76 ☎ 417.337.9539 🖑 andywilliams.com) This restaurant sits on the grounds of Andy Williams' Moon River Theater and is owned by the famous tenor. Though this is by no means fine dining, the atmosphere does have an upscale feel. Andy is an art collector, and pieces by Andy Warhol, David Sheridan, and Donald Roller are on display. So are Andy's gold and platinum records, and there are quite a few. Andy's music plays in the background except when there is live entertainment at the piano.

While the restaurant has a chic feel, menu offerings are more like what your mother would have answered when you asked what was for dinner. In fact, the chicken pot pie, meatloaf, and pot roast are made from Andy's mother's recipes. In addition, there are burgers, salads, steaks, and fish. With names like Naughty Betty and Sex on the Moon, the bar menu may bring some laughs even before having a drink. ($$-$$$)

THE RIVERSTONE RESTAURANT
(24 Downing St., Hollister ☎ 417.544.9056

☗ oldenglishinnhollister.com) Located next to Ye Olde English Inn, the Riverstone restaurant is an experience as much as a place to eat. It's just a few minutes' drive from Branson, but seems to be locked in another lifetime. Because this area of historic downtown Hollister was the last stop for the railroad, it began to be advertised as a hunting and fishing destination. Inside are plaster molds of real fish caught when the building was constructed in 1909.

A rich breakfast menu has something for every appetite including biscuits and gravy, eggs and bacon, pastries, quiche and breakfast sandwiches. Lunch includes a selection of gourmet sandwiches, soups and salads. A home-style dinner menu features meatloaf, chicken fried steak, angus burgers and more. ($$)

UPTOWN CAFE
(285 Hwy 165 S ☎ 417.336.3535 ☗ bransonuptowncafe.com)
No one can miss the Uptown Cafe just across from the Titanic Museum. The distinctive architecture and the yellow taxi in front of this 50s-style diner will grab anyone's attention. Inside, there's rock and roll music from a real jukebox and ice cream from an old-time soda fountain. The menu includes

steakburgers, fish and chips, chili, sandwiches, and more. Kids' meals are a little pricey, but most of the menu is reasonable.

The Uptown opens early for breakfast and stays open late. It's not unusual to find a show going on here; the music may be anything from George Strait to Barry Manilow. ($$)

ITALIAN/PIZZA

Great Italian can be found in the Ozarks. Whether it's a sit-down lasagna meal or pizza delivered to the hotel there is a nice variety from which to choose.

FLORENTINA'S

(2690 Green Mountain Dr. ☎ 417.337.9882
florentinasristoranteitaliano.com) This centrally located restaurant is close to the Strip behind the Grand Palace Theatre. The atmosphere is relaxed and comfortable, the Italian decor tasteful. On some days there is a photographer who will take pictures at your table for a fee.

Florentina's offers a number of appetizers and salads, including an excellent warm spinach salad. Besides all of the classic pasta dishes, there are steak and seafood entrées. Some items are available as side dishes, from meatballs to broccoli and green beans. McFarlain's also offers a unique and economical option with a variety of family platters. ($$)

MR. G'S CHICAGO STYLE PIZZA

(202½ N Commercial St. ☎ 417.335.8156) You could easily miss Mr. G's if you weren't looking for it. This is a little "hole in the wall" restaurant around the corner from Chappy Mall.

The atmosphere is a little smoky, with booth seats that have been around a while, framed pictures of sports figures on the wall, and televisions placed around the restaurant.

Mr. G's is a local hangout. The pizza is well seasoned, and there's no skimping on toppings. Mr. G's Favorite combines all sorts of meats and vegetables. The Chicago-style pizza comes served in its deep-dish pan. Everything is homemade, which means it may take a while to be served. To bide the time, try the Tony Orlando Salad, with pepperoni, olives, mushrooms, cheese, and a homemade Italian dressing. ($-$$)

PIZZA WORLD ✪ Must See!
(3405 W Hwy 76 ☎ 417.337.7778 🖊 pizzaworldusa.net) For a quick and satisfying bite, Pizza World cannot be beat. In addition to pizza, there are calzone, sandwiches (the hot Italian sub is highly recommended), salads, and dessert pizzas. A pizza buffet is also available. Pizza World will deliver to your hotel room. Check online for coupons. ($-$$)

ROCKY'S ITALIAN RESTAURANT
(120 N Sycamore St. ☎ 417.335.4765) Walking into Rocky's is walking into Branson history. This local favorite is more than a hundred years old. The menu proudly reads, "To all who enter, Cento annni pen sembra," which translates "One hundred years forever." The wooden floors, private booths, and antiques enhance the historic feel. Among a variety of collections the owner displays is a unique assortment of old-fashioned scales. Paintings by local artists also adorn the walls.

Rocky's signature salad is a nice way to begin a meal. It comes with dinner entrées. There are plenty of appetizers and a nice beer and wine selection. Entrées include pastas, seafood, chicken, beef, and veal. The food is good although not necessarily the best Italian to be found in Branson. The dessert is another story: the tiramisu is some of the best anywhere. A full bar is connected to the restaurant, and there's impressive live entertainment on the weekends. Larger groups can use a separate dining room. Reservations are recommended. ($$)

MEXICAN

There are several Mexican restaurants around town but many locals recommend these favorite spots.

CANTINA LAREDO ⭐ Must See!
(1001 Branson Landing Blvd. ☎ 417.334.6062
🖱 **cantinalaredo.com)** Ask a local where to find the best Mexican food, and chances are they'll say Cantina Laredo. The atmosphere here is upscale, with tablecloths, comfortable booths, and a circular bar in the center of the restaurant. An outdoor patio offers views of Lake Taneycomo and the opportunity to watch Branson Landing's water fountain display while you dine. The food is fresh and of high quality. Guacamole is made tableside. The menu offers a large selection of classic Mexican fare like fajitas, chili rellenos, enchiladas, and tacos, along with fish, chicken, and steak. Good Mexican food isn't easily found in Missouri, but you can find it at Cantina Laredo. ($$-$$$)

CASA FUENTES
(1107 W Hwy 76 ☎ 417.339.3888 🖱 casafuentes.com) Having just celebrated its 15th anniversary this Mexican restaurant has stood the test of time. It's easy to miss this small place located

on the east end of the strip. While it has just 42 seats Casa Fuentes has gained popularity over the years with both locals and tourists. Favorites are the gringas (marinated steak taco), enchiladas verdes and margaritas. There is additional seating on the back patio when weather permits. ($)

ASIAN

There are several Asian restaurants in town but not all are memorable. Thai Thai Cuisine is highly recommended. For those craving a good Chinese buffet, The Great Wall will not disappoint.

GREAT WALL CHINESE SUPER BUFFET

(1315 Highway 76 ☎ 417.334.8838) The Great Wall Chinese Super Buffet features four large stations filled with every kind of Chinese food a person could want. Start off with a variety of fruits, soups and salads and move on to crispy chicken (or beef/pork) with a choice of sauces. On the side choose egg rolls, shrimp, steamed or fried rice, crab rangoon and fried bread. Patrons can also create their own dish with the restaurant's Mongolian Barbeque option. Choose your own meat, vegetables and sauce to make your own palette-pleasing entrée. For dessert, there are plenty of choices including soft serve ice cream, cream puffs, cakes, and cookies.

THAI THAI CUISINE ✪ Must See!

(1615 W Hwy 76, Suite H-I ☎ 417.334.9070) Those who are familiar with Thai food will be thrilled with the freshness and quality of this restaurant's cuisine. For those who aren't, this is a good place to try it. The restaurant is tastefully decorated, with large, private booths, wooden floors, and pleasant lighting.

The menu includes traditional favorites, and diners can have spice levels adjusted to their tastes. If you're looking for something not on the menu, Thai Thai most likely can make it. The panang curry, flavorful with kaffir leaf and coconut milk, is served over fresh spinach. The sweet and cold Thai coffee or tea is excellent. For dessert, the mango and sticky rice will not disappoint. For a change of pace, Thai Thai Cuisine is highly recommended. ($$)

SEAFOOD

There are several seafood restaurants in town. For a more casual experience try Joe's Crab Shack at the Branson Landing. Still casual but a little more upscale is Landry's on the strip.

JOE'S CRAB SHACK

(717 Branson Landing ☎ 417.337.7373 ◉ joescrabshack.com)
This popular restaurant on Branson Landing can have long waits, so families will appreciate the large playground in front. Inside, there are large wooden booths and tables, with tall windows offering lots of light and views of Lake Taneycomo.

Joe's is, of course, known for its crab. There's a range of seafood dishes, plus salads, burgers, and a nice choice of sides. A fun selection of margaritas is available, along with beer and other drinks. ($-$$)

LANDRY'S SEAFOOD HOUSE

(2900 W. Hwy 76 ☎ 417.339.1010 ◉ landrysseafood.com)
Landry's is a casual fine-dining steak and seafood chain with more than 20 locations across the country. You can't miss its

theater-style marquee lighting up the center of the Strip. Inside, there are white tablecloths and lots of large windows. Dark wood and brick accent a fishing mural on one wall. A tank of live lobster promises a really fresh meal.

The clam chowder is excellent, and the fish selections are always good choices. The steak is also popular. The kids' menu is pricier than at many restaurants but offers a nice variety. There is a tempting assortment of desserts, many of them big enough to share. ($$)

WHIPPER SNAPPERS
(2421 W Hwy 76 ☎ 417.334.3282
☗ bransonsbestrestaurant.com) Whipper Snappers is a highly advertised restaurant in Branson, but the food doesn't live up to the advertising. An overwhelming fish odor greets you at the entrance to the restaurant, which is located on the ground floor of Peppercorn restaurant. The seafood buffet includes all-you-can-eat lobster and crab, but the taste is a letdown. This is an expensive buffet that simply isn't worth the price. There is a menu offered for those not interested in the buffet. ($$-$$$)

WHITE RIVER FISH HOUSE
(1 Bass Pro Dr ☎ 417.243.5100
☗ restaurants.basspro.com/whiteriverfishhouse) Walk in the door of the White River Fish House and it's obvious this is a Bass Pro business. Impressive fish occupy a giant tank; canoes hang from the ceiling while antique fishing pictures and regalia adorn the walls. A huge fireplace offers a rustic ambiance. The building itself is actually a barge, floating on Lake Taneycomo. Floor to ceiling windows provide satisfying views of the water while dining.

It's tempting to fill up on the complimentary – and oh-so-good cornbread - but leave room for appetizers. This is the place to have that first taste of alligator. The alligator tail appetizer is sweet and spicy and altogether delicious. Another unique and tasty appetizer is the smoked wahoo dip. The recipe comes straight from Jeannie Morris, wife of Bass Pro founder, Johnny Morris.

The main course (and dessert for that matter) won't disappoint, either. The Ozarks Trout Almondine is recognized as one of the top trout dishes in the area. For those opposed to fish there are pasta, steak, chicken and burger options. But, really, you'll want to try the fish. ($$)

STEAK

There are a number of excellent steak restaurants in Branson. Level 2 is perfect for those looking for an exquisite fine dining experience. The Golden Corral buffet offers all you can eat steak cooked to order.

BUCKINGHAM'S
(2820 W Hwy 76 ☎ 417.334.7666

🖰 clarionhotelbranson.com/restaurants.asp?menu=buckinghams)
This casual yet somewhat upscale restaurant is located in the Clarion Hotel next to the Grand Palace Theatre. Its jungle theme is a nod to famed English hunter Sir Buckingham. At one time the menu featured alligator and other wild game, but nowadays Buckingam's is known for its prime rib. Other favorites include bourbon-glazed pork shanks; the meat on these beauties literally falls off the bone. Before your main dish, the

Shrimp Diablo appetizer is recommended for its wonderful sauce. The kids' menu offers a nice selection.

Buckingham's features tableside services for preparation of several of its dishes: Caesar Salad, Steak Dianne, Seafood Pasta, and Elegant Raspberries à la Buckingham. ($$-$$$)

FALL CREEK STEAK & CATFISH HOUSE
(997 Hwy 165 ☎ 417.336.5060 🍴 bransonsbestrestaurant.com)
This large restaurant just south of the Strip is hard to miss, with its huge steer facing traffic and its restaurant sign flanking either side. Inside, long lines of tables are nice for large groups. This restaurant claims to be the original home of the "tossed roll." The rolls are hot and definitely enjoyable but not in the same league as those at Lambert's in Ozark, regardless of who began throwing them first.

Large road signs and other antique memorabilia adorn the walls. Big windows look out onto Fall Creek, offering ample natural light. Patrons can order the buffet or eat off the menu, with choices ranging from appetizers and salads to steak, catfish, and burgers. The food and service are decent but not spectacular. ($$-$$$)

MONTANA MIKE'S
(3225 W. Hwy 76 ☎ 417.334.2766, 1464 Hwy 248
☎ 417.334.5893 🍴 bransonimax.com) Montana Mike's has two locations, one on the Strip next to the Titanic Museum and the other on Highway 248 across from Kmart. There's enough on the menu to please everyone, and enough on the plate to feed anyone. For the really hungry (or really crazy), there's even a 44-ounce steak waiting to be ordered. Eat the whole thing

and get a free t-shirt. Whatever the entrée, be sure to have the onion soup; this is onion soup heaven. Chicken is tender and tasty, and you won't go wrong ordering one of the 21-day naturally aged steaks. Kids can order off their own menu and then color it in. The restaurant's bar has a 50-inch plasma television and happy hour half-price drinks and appetizers Monday through Friday from 2 to 7 p.m. ($$-$$$)

OUTBACK STEAK AND OYSTER BAR

(1914 W Hwy 76 ☎ 417.334.0005 ⬤ outbackbranson.com) This has the look of other Outback Steakhouse restaurants, but since it is not a franchise, not everything is the same. It has the same rugged outdoor feel, starting with the full-sized (though not real) crocodile outside. Inside, the atmosphere is casual and comfortable. There is a porch for dining outside in nice weather.

In addition to steak, the menu includes alligator tail, oysters, shrimp, chicken, lamb, and pork dishes. Sandwiches and burgers are available for lunch. A kids' menu even includes shrimp for an additional fee. The food here is good but seems a little pricey for the quality and atmosphere. The pub next door features a smaller version of the restaurant menu. ($$-$$$)

TEXAS LAND & CATTLE

(915 Branson Landing Blvd. ☎ 417.337.8200 ⬤ txlc.com) The smell alone can wake up an appetite walking into Texas Land and Cattle. The atmosphere is eclectic, with comfortable booths and patio seating on the waterfront when weather is favorable.

There's really not a bad choice on the menu, but the smoked sirloin is exceptional. The meat, smoked to your preference, never touches a grill. Best of all, you can try a sample before ordering. Other items include signature salads, chicken, ribs, and shrimp. A kids' menu includes, along with the typical fare, steak medallions and grilled chicken with broccoli. Desserts are huge but worth it. ($$-$$$)

FINE DINING

When looking for a place to celebrate a special occasion there are a number of outstanding options in Branson. Diners can choose a lake view table, a romantic fireside meal, the ambiance of the Chateau or soothing live entertainment at the historical Worman House. Any of these restaurants will provide the right backdrop for meaningful occasions.

CANDLESTICK INN ✪ Must See!

(127 Taney St. ☎ 417.334.3633 ◖ candlestickinn.com) This is hands down one of the most beautiful views to be found in Branson. Across the lake from Branson Landing, Candlestick Inn sits high on a hill overlooking Lake Taneycomo and the lights of the Landing. The Inn has a rustic yet elegant feel, with its white tablecloths and soft lighting. Full-length windows give diners breathtaking views at sunset. During warmer months, patio dining is also available.

Opened in 1962, this restaurant has changed hands several times but has remained family owned, and the camaraderie of the management and staff is evident. They call Candlestick Inn a "casual fine-dining experience." Specialties include pan-seared scallops and an elk rack with a ground mushroom beurre blanc. Steaks and seafood are also featured. Starch and vegetable choices change every evening. An upstairs lounge features the same menu and service in an even more relaxed atmosphere.

The Candlestick is open for dinner only, beginning at 5 p.m. It is closed on Mondays and during the month of January. ($$-$$$)

CHATEAU GRILLE
(415 N Hwy 265 ☎ 417.334.1161
☗ chateauonthelakebranson.com) Enjoy views of Table Rock Lake from inside this elegant dining room located inside the Chateau on the Lake. Open for breakfast, lunch, and dinner, the Chateau Grill offers a memorable dining experience whether it's a family occasion or romantic meal for two. Unique about this restaurant is its Chef's Table where diners glean from the chef's recipes and knowledge. A private dining room is also available with a custom menu for those wanting a truly first class experience. Reservations are required for the Chef's Table and the private dining room. Outdoor seating is available when weather permits. ($$$)

LEVEL 2 STEAKHOUSE ✪ Must See!
(Hilton Convention Center, 200 E. Main St. ☎ 417.243.3433
☗ level2steakhouse.com) A fine-dining experience here begins with complimentary valet parking. This intimate restaurant—a fine choice for celebrating a special occasion—boasts a quiet atmosphere with contemporary yet comfortable decor. In the warmer months, the summer salad with Missouri goat cheese, toasted coconut, fresh fruit, candied walnuts, and vanilla vinaigrette gets a top recommendation. Most of the produce

is locally grown. The corn-fed Hereford beef is aged 28 days and cooked in a 1,600-degree infrared oven. Everything on the plate is homemade: sauces, the egg noodles with delectable five-cheese sauce, and the whipped cream to go with the chef's signature butter cake.

Level 2 is reputedly the only restaurant in southwest Missouri to have a staff sommelier, which assists diners with wine selection on Friday and Saturday nights. Also unique to Level 2 is its "cut club." Diners choose from a variety of steak knives, and after a fifth visit the knife is engraved with the diner's name and saved for future meals. ($-$$$)

STEVE'S TREEHOUSE

(50 Stonebridge Pkwy, Branson West ☎ 417.239.0445
🌐 stevestreehouse.com) Steve's Treehouse is a beautiful restaurant with a large stone fireplace in its center and tall windows letting in lots of natural light and providing a beautiful view. The Sunday brunch is outstanding. The dinner menu features seafood and steak selections as well as prime rib. Steve's Treehouse is closed during the month of January. ($$-$$$)

WORMAN HOUSE

(Big Cedar Lodge, 612 Devils Pool Rd., Ridgedale
☎ 417.339.5200 🌐 bigcedar.com) The inspiring view, linen-clad tables, and atmospheric lighting of Worman House classify it as a fine-dining restaurant, and it's a worthy choice for any special occasion. Still, families need not shy away. The menu features a wide price range, and there's a kids' menu. Choices include a Black Angus burger that sets a new standard when it comes to burgers. Other favorites include the fried chicken, salmon, filet, and pork. The recipe for the gooey butter cake

comes from Big Cedar (and Bass Pro founder) owner Johnny Morris' mother. You will want to thank her after eating this decadent cake.

Originally the home of wealthy railroad businessman Harold Worman, the house was built in anticipation of the soon-to-be Table Rock Lake. Worman and his young wife, Dorothy, lived here until the end of their marriage in the 1930s. Rumors of murder surrounded Dorothy's death, and ever since there have been supposed sightings of her ghost. (She's probably just looking for a taste of the butter cake.)

The Worman House is open for dinner and Sunday brunch. Live entertainment is featured most nights; the schedule is limited in the winter. Reservations are recommended. ($$-$$$)

BARS/CLUBS

Nightlife is alive and well in Branson. These spots are good choices for drinks and entertainment after the show.

THE BLACK HORSE PUB

(24 Downing St., Hollister ☎ 417.334.4888) This small and quaint pub is just a short drive from Branson in downtown Hollister. The pub and nearby Old English Inn and River Stone Restaurant are all owned by romance author Janet Dailey, who gave the pub its name because of her love of horses. In addition to drinks, The Black Horse serves burgers and appetizers, including quesadillas, queso, guacamole, buffalo wings, bruschetta, and even fried pickles. The pub features local entertainment and karaoke. ($$)

THE BUZZARD BAR

(Big Cedar Lodge, 612 Devils Pool Rd., Ridgedale
☎ **417.335.2777** 🍸 **bigcedar.com)** The Buzzard Bar at Big
Cedar Lodge has great drinks and entertainment. Clay Self,
otherwise known as "The Singing Cowboy," has been featured
on the Grand Ole Opry stage and has a voice that rivals any
country singer heard on the radio—and he's hilarious. The
comedy mixed with fine country music is a Branson show in
itself. There's a full menu of appetizers and main courses. Fried
chicken gizzards and fried green tomatoes are among favorite
appetizers. Frozen and hot drinks, margaritas, daiquiris, and
pina coladas are all available; Dorothy's Revenge is a favorite
among the regulars. ($$)

CLUB 57 ✪ Must See!

(Dick Clark's American Bandstand Theatre, 1600 W. Hwy 76
☎ **417.339.3003** 🍸 **dickclarksabbranson.com/club57.html)** This
is a hands-down favorite when it comes to Branson night-
life. Club 57 is in the downstairs portion of the American
Bandstand Theatre, and it's nice to be able to simply go down-
stairs for a drink after watching a show. Occasionally the stars
do the same. It's not uncommon for musicians from Legends
in Concert and other shows around town to take the stage—no
choreographed numbers here, just great music.

This is a spacious club with good food and drinks and a lively
atmosphere. There's a dance floor right in front of the band.
Club 57 has karaoke and live music Thursday, Friday, and
Saturday nights. ($$)

ERNIE BIGGS DUELING PIANO BAR AND GRILLE

(505 Branson Landing Blvd. ☎ 417.239.3670
⬤ branson.erniebiggs.com) This is a fun place to hang out
with friends and enjoy food, drinks, and entertainment. The
piano players can perform just about any song that might be
requested. There's a large menu of appetizers, salads, burgers,
and sandwiches with names like the Ray Charles, the Barry
Manilow, and the Beefy Joel. The drinks list is just as long.
There is a cover charge. ($-$$)

OUTBACK PUB

(1914 W Hwy 76 ☎ 417.334.0005 ⬤ outbackbranson.com)
Located just off the Strip, this club sits on the same property
as Outback Steak and Oyster Bar. The pub is one of the few
places in Branson that stays open past midnight. A covered
porch is enjoyable during nice weather. The pub serves appetizers and sandwiches along with more than a hundred kinds
of beer and other drinks. There is live entertainment every
night. It can be pretty loud and crowded on the weekends, with
bands on the deck and in the lounge. ($$)

ROWDY BEAVER

(1810 W. Hwy 76 ☎ 417.334.7409 ⬤ rowdybeaver.com) Those
looking for a place to eat late, perhaps after a show, can find
it here. This spacious and rustic restaurant and tavern is open
until midnight, and you might even get a live performance
from country music singer Johnny Lee, who shows up on occa-
sion. There are bands every weekend and karaoke on some
nights. The music is a mix of genres, nothing too extreme. The
restaurant specializes in steaks and also offers seafood and a
kids' menu. On some days a buffet is served. Rowdy Beaver is
a favorite Branson nightlife spot. ($-$$)

Historic Downtown Branson

Strolling the area officially known as Historic Downtown Branson feels like stepping back in time. The brick-lined sidewalks and old-fashioned lampposts make a quaint and peaceful shopping setting. There's an old-time five and dime store, and more than a hundred other businesses offer everything from clocks to cowboy gear, Victoriana to veterans' items.

The free **Discovery Trolley** *(*🖰 *downtownbranson.org/ trolley)* transports shoppers throughout the downtown district. Wait times are usually no more than 15 minutes, and benches throughout the area are nice for relaxing during the wait. The trolley runs from 8 a.m. to 6 p.m. every day except Thanksgiving and Christmas. Complimentary maps with route information are available in most downtown businesses. For a more romantic memory, opt for a horse-drawn carriage ride instead. Board the carriage at North Commercial and Atlantic streets. Rides are $10 per adult for a 20 minute ride, $20 for a 40 minute ride. Kids are half-price. Contact **Branson Carriage Rides** *(*☎ *417.593.1958)* for information.

THEATERS

Two downtown theaters offer live entertainment. Both have limited schedules; call or check online for current information.

BRANSON HOT HITS THEATRE
(206 S Commercial St. ☎ 417.337.7426 🖰 bransonhothits.com)
Watching a show in this 84-seat theatre is almost like sitting in an entertainer's living room thanks to its smaller size. Entering

the building feels a little like walking into an old-time diner thanks to the coffee shop lobby. Here guests can enjoy many specialty coffee house drinks and even a sandwich. The theatre is busy with five to seven shows running throughout any given year. Regulars include Motown Downtown, a Hank Williams and Patsy Cline tribute and Breakfast with Mark Twain. Guests attending this show eat across the street at Downtown Diner before enjoying the theatre performance. Call for a current listing and group pricing. ($)

OWENS THEATRE

(205 S Commercial St. ☎ 417.336.1113) Some say this was the first theater in Branson. It was built in 1936 by Mayor Jim Owen as a movie theater and is now completely remodeled to seat more than 200 people for live performances. It's believed that John Wayne attended the premiere of *The Shepherd of the Hills* in this theater. More ghostly rumors have the spirit of Rose O'Neal—creator of the Kewpie doll—haunting the place, since she was said to be a frequent visitor.

DINING DOWNTOWN

Eat downtown at some of Branson's oldest establishments, like the Branson Café or the Farmhouse Family Restaurant, or experience the newer side of things with nearby Branson Landing restaurants. From fine dining to fudge, it's all available on the tree-lined streets of the downtown area.

BRANSON LANDING

(100 Branson Landing ☎ 417.239.3002 ☷ bransonlanding.com)
One of the newer additions to Branson, this outdoor mall offers shops, restaurants, department stores, and even concerts. A Bass Pro shop anchors one end of the mall, a Belk department store the other. In between are more than 100 stores, including national clothing chains, children's stores, and jewelry and accessory shops.

Shopping here feels like shopping on a boardwalk. The Landing sits next to Lake Taneycomo and, in addition to shopping, offers special attractions and entertainment. The most prominent feature is the $7.5 million water fountain show. A lineup of fountains shoots water 120 feet into the air, synchronized with cannons shooting flames. Light and music are choreographed with the action for an impressive performance against the backdrop of the lake. Shows usually begin at the top of every hour beginning at noon, with special patriotic performances at designated times. There's a large, terrace-like seating area.

When the kids start getting restless, take them over to the playground at Joe's Crab Shack. It's a nice place to relax right in the center of the Landing.

The Hilton Promenade at Branson Landing allows people to literally sleep at the mall, and the Hilton Branson Convention Center is right across the street. Condominiums on Branson Landing can also be rented through the Hilton Promenade for longer stays.

GUEST SERVICES

Check in at guest services for a map of the complex and a coupon booklet. There are three locations throughout the Landing. Free soda, popcorn, and balloons for the kids are always offered, and this is also the place to go for free wheelchairs and electric scooters.

BRANSON LANDING DINING

The Landing offers numerous meal options. Joe's Crab Shack serves good seafood, and its atmosphere is casual enough for the whole family. Another good seafood choice is the White River Fish House. Other possibilities include popular chain restaurants like Macaroni Grill and Old Chicago and more upscale eateries like Cantina Laredo, a favorite Mexican restaurant among locals. Steak and barbecue lovers can head for Texas Land and Cattle or Famous Dave's. For nightlife, Ernie Biggs Dueling Piano Bar and Grille stays open late, serving up a full menu, drinks, and entertainment. Want to combine a meal with sightseeing? Try Branson Landing Cruises for lunch or dinner outings on Lake Taneycomo.

Shopping

Outlet centers, gift shops, antique stores, craft shops, and outdoor malls are all part of the Branson area shopping experience. You'll find handcrafted items and Christmas decorations along with clothing, souvenirs, and fishing gear—and just about anything else you're looking for.

BASS PRO SHOPS

(1935 S. Campbell, Springfield ☎ 417.887.7334 ⬤ basspro.com)
Bass Pro hardly needs an introduction. As the official headquarters of the outdoor chain, the 40,000-square-foot store in Springfield is "mecca" for many. It has everything, literally every thing, one might need for outdoor sport and recreation.

The spacious, rustic-style facility isn't just for shopping. This is an entertaining place to take the kids to see indoor waterfalls, aquariums filled with enormous fish, and wildlife exhibits. As much museum as store, Bass Pro can be an all-day experience. There is a boat showroom and a wilderness museum on the property. There's a wood-burning fireplace inside the Grand Entrance with rocking chairs for those who prefer to sit and relax.

Bass Pro holds a number of special events throughout the year. At Christmastime, kids can come here to write a letter to Santa and have their picture taken with him, free of charge.

There is also a Bass Pro location at the Branson Landing shopping center.

BRANSON CRAFT MALL

(694 Hwy 165 ☎ 417.334.1223 ⬢ bransoncraftmall.com) This mall is exactly what its name indicates. Shoppers will find unique souvenirs and gifts here, and often there's the chance to watch artists at work. The mall features hundreds of arts and crafts booths. Guys may opt for the men's "sittin' room" while their companions shop. There are candles, baskets, pottery, brass engravings, woodwork, and even handmade musical instruments.

DICK'S 5 & 10 ✪ Must See!

(103 W Main St. ☎ 417.334.2410 ⬢ dicksoldtime5and10.com) Time seems to have stood still on the downtown corner where Dick's 5 & 10 is located. From the old-fashioned sign on top of the building to the wooden counters inside, Dick's is a living remnant of another era. In business for more than 50 years, the family-owned store has more than 50,000 items for sale. Fascinating collections on display include more than a hundred autographed aviation prints of the Black Sheep Squadron, the Flying Tigers, the Enola Gay, and even Luftwaffe planes. There are arrowhead and train collections and autographed portraits of Baseball Hall of Fame players.

This store still does business the old-fashioned way: there's no computer here, but there is friendly service and plenty of unique items to fill at least a couple of the tiny shopping carts.

GRAND VILLAGE

(2800 W. Hwy 76 ☎ 417.336.4300 ⬢ grandvillageshops.com) Grand Village is right on the Strip next to the Grand Palace Theatre. This outdoor mall has a completely different feel than anything else in town. Its design is patterned after the historic district of Charleston, South Carolina, with brick-lined streets framed by attractive landscaping and classic architecture.

Grand Village features a beautiful Christmas store and specialty shops selling toys, jewelry, gifts, and art. At Christmas, Santa can usually be found shopping here. In the center of the village, a gigantic rocking chair presents a photo opportunity that's hard to resist; not even Dad's feet will reach the edge of the chair. Dining options include Sugar Leaf Treats, offering soups, salads, and sweets, and the popular Hard Luck Diner.

TANGER OUTLET CENTER

(300 Tanger Blvd., Ste 120 ☎ 800.407.2762
☷ **tangeroutlet.com/branson)** This outdoor mall is filled with major chain stores and specialty shops offering everything from kids' and adult clothing to shoes, accessories, and house-wares. There is also a small selection of fast dining choices.

Branson Landing offers shops, restaurants, department stores, and even concerts.

Lakes

⬦——————————————————————————————————————⭐

The White River changed forever with the creation of Bull Shoals, Powersite and Table Rock Dams. Now three large and very distinct bodies of water stand against the backdrop of the Ozark mountains. The lakes draw both championship and amateur fishermen along with every kind of water sport enthusiast. Families return to these lakes year after year adding new memories of swimming, boating, fishing and lakeside barbeques.

BULL SHOALS LAKE

The last in the chain of area lakes, **Bull Shoals** (⬦ *bullshoals.com*) is about an hour's drive south from Branson. It snakes its way from Forsyth southward into Arkansas, with wide-open channels and tons of finger-like coves offering great fishing and privacy. There are more than 700 miles of shoreline, most of it rugged and undeveloped. It's not uncommon to see wildlife. Still, there are several public swimming beaches and marinas to accommodate water enthusiasts. Bull Shoals boasts the fifth largest dam in the United States which is found just north of Cotter, Arkansas.

The water at Bull Shoals is clear and almost always smooth, making it ideal for fishing, swimming, and scuba diving. Scuba gear can be rented at several marinas, and lessons are available. Bass fishermen are drawn to Bull Shoals for its white, largemouth, and spotted bass. Crappie, bream, and catfish are also plentiful. Several pro and amateur fishing tournaments are held on the lake, and there's an eagle awareness weekend every July. A popular fireworks display takes place at the dam on the Fourth of July.

BULL SHOALS BOAT DOCKS AND MARINAS

Whether storing or renting a boat, fishing on your own or finding a guide, Bull Shoals boat docks and marinas have it all.

BULL SHOALS LAKE BOAT DOCK

(Bull Shoals Lake Boat Dock, 719 Shorecrest Drive Bull Shoals, AR ☎ 870.445.4424 🖱 bullshoalslakeboatdock.com) Bull Shoals Lake Boat Dock has everything from houseboat to waverunner rentals. They have scuba gear, a bait and tackle shop, guided fishing and even campsites. This marina is about an hour-and-a-half from Branson near the Arkansas White River.

K DOCK MARINA

(727 Warren Rd., Kirbyville ☎ 417.334.2880 🖱 kdockmarina.com) Located just eight miles from Branson on the northwest part of Bull Shoals Lake, this is a full service marina. K Dock also has the seasonal "Bait Shop Restaurant" which serves breakfast and lunch.

SUGAR LOAF HARBOR MARINA

(1502 Shore Line Dr. Lead Hill, AR ☎ 870.422.2900 🖱 sugarloafharbormarina.com) Sugar Loaf Marina is a little more than an hour's drive south of Branson near Highway 14. They claim to be the most secure marina with all steel docks, gated entry, and video security. Their rental boats are new and so is the marina's store.

TABLE ROCK LAKE

Table Rock Lake came into being in 1958 with the completion of Table Rock Dam on the White River six miles southwest of Branson. Fishermen were already well familiar with the White River's abundance, but the dam was needed to help prevent flooding. It also serves as a source of power. Table Rock Lake encompasses more than 43,000 surface acres, with more than 750 miles of shoreline.

Recognized as a top bass fishing lake, this is a fisherman's playground. There are largemouth, smallmouth, and almost every other kind of bass, and also catfish of every size, bluegill, and crappie. Tackle them alone or hire a fishing guide. For those looking for a little competition, there are tournaments throughout the year.

Beyond fishing, there are full-service marinas and more than a hundred private resorts providing boats for every type of excursion. Specialized cruises are also available, including dinner shows on the Showboat Branson Belle. Those who don't want to be on the water can enjoy its pristine scenery from lakeside restaurants. There are also a number of lodging choices along the lake.

MOONSHINE BEACH

(3778 S. Hwy 165 ☎ 417.335.8383) Moonshine Beach, owned and operated by the U.S. Army Corp of Engineers, is located just north of the dam. It is the only sand swimming beach on Table Rock Lake. Moonshine Beach offers a picnic area, swimming, volleyball, a playground, and a boat launch. There are also bathrooms and outdoor showers. A small entrance fee is charged per car.

TABLE ROCK LAKE BOAT DOCKS AND MARINAS

Boat docks and marinas are plentiful around all of the Ozarks lakes. Whether visitors are looking to jet ski, take the family on a pontoon or bass fish with a buddy, plenty of large facilities and small, family run businesses are ready with the needed equipment.

INDIAN POINT MARINA

(3443 Indian Point Rd. ☎ 417.338.2891

☝ **indianpointmarina.com)** This full-service marina at Table Rock Lake has a large selection of boats and wave runners. Docks are available for short and long term storage. The marina is also equipped with a small gas station and store where you can purchase fishing licenses, snacks and other lake necessities. A dive center is also located on site and offers training for those wanting some underwater adventure.

The marina's Floating Café is a popular spot for vacationers with its newly renovated building and casual fare. It's open early for breakfast and continues to serve through dinner during the peak season.

Indian Point Marina is a short drive from the strip but the atmosphere gives it the feeling you are more secluded. In fact, you're actually just a few miles from Silver Dollar City!

STATE PARK MARINA

(380 State Park Marina Rd. ☎ 417.334.2628

☍ **boatbranson.com)** This large marina at Table Rock State Park near the dam offers ski, deck, pontoon, luxury, and bass boats. It also has WaveRunners, scuba instruction, and parasailing. Ninety-minute, two-hour, and sunset cruises are available on the 48-foot sailing catamaran Spirit of America. There is also a swim play tour where the boat parks in a cove and allows riders to play on various inflatable play equipment.

WHAT'S UP DOCK

(49 Lake Rd., Kimberling City ☎ 417.739.4511 ☍ mypok.com) Located just 15 miles west of Branson, What's Up Dock is the largest dock in Missouri. In fact, it's one of the largest in the country. Part of the Port of Kimberling Resort, it offers an extensive list of boat and WaveRunner rentals. Many families, both large and small come back year after year to rent their luxurious houseboats. (Plan to reserve houseboats four to six months in advance.) More than 1300 slips (wet slips and dry stack storage) are also available through Port of Kimberling.

Coyotes Dockside Café has recently expanded and now includes a full service menu as well as an ice cream parlor. Patrons can pull up by car or by boat to dine on steak, crab legs or a quick sandwich.

LAKE TANEYCOMO

The 1913 opening of the Powersite Dam on the White River near Forsyth created 22-mile-long Lake Taneycomo, the state's first man-made lake. (Taneycomo is short for Taney County

Missouri.) Officials thought it would take about six months for the more than 2,000 acres to fill, but torrential rains caused the reservoir to fill in just two days, creating the largest body of water between the Mississippi and the Rockies.

When Table Rock Dam was completed in 1958, the cold bottom waters of Table Rock Lake flowed into Taneycomo and changed it from a warmwater lake to a coldwater lake.. But the frigid temperatures that made Taneycomo too chilly for swimmers created the perfect conditions for rainbow and brown trout. The Missouri Department of Conservation envisioned this and, two years before the dam was completed, opened the Shepherd of the Hills Fish Hatchery. To this day the hatchery keeps Taneycomo well stocked with coldwater fish. The lake has a reputation for some of the finest trout fishing in the world.

When fishing near the Table Rock Dam, it's important to know that when a horn blows it means power is about to be generated. This affects Taneycomo's currents and water depth; the water can rise very quickly. Most of the Lake Taneycomo shoreline is private property, so bank fishing must be done from a public park or trout dock.

TANEYCOMO BOAT DOCKS AND MARINAS

Taneycomo marinas offer boating and fishing gear as well as expert fishing guides.

LILLEY'S LANDING RESORT AND MARINA

(367 River Ln. ☎ 417.334.6380 📱 lilleyslanding.com) Lilley's Landing is one of the few marinas on Lake Taneycomo. It's a family-run operation, and the Lilleys—who've been here for nearly three decades—are always available to answer questions, especially when it comes to fishing. Pontoons, jon boats, and bass boats are available to rent here. There are three fish-cleaning stations, one of them heated to make it comfortable in winter, since Lilley's is open year-round.

SCOTTY'S TROUT DOCK AND MARINA
(400 South Boxcar Willie Dr. ☎ 417.334.4288

📱 scottystroutdock.com) Family fun and family fishing is the focus of Scotty's. The family-owned operation provides guided pontoon trips for up to six people. Bass, pontoon and other fishing boats are available for rent.

FISHING GUIDES AND SERVICES

The Branson Lakes area offers some of the best fresh water fishing in the country. There are more than 200 species of fish waiting to be caught. Trout and bass fishing are among the most popular here. Novice and experienced fishermen appreciate the opportunity to improve their skills with a guide service. Whether its fly or trout fishing there is a guide service available for every kind of fishing adventure. For a copy of the latest fishing regulations from the Missouri Department of Conservation call ☎ 800.781.1989.

Fishing services and guides are available at numerous locations, including: **Branson Fishing Guide Service** *(177 Boston Drive, Ridgedale* ☎ *417.270.7157* 📱 *bransonfishingguideservice.com)* **Lilleys's Landing Resort and Marina** *(367 River Ln.* ☎ *417.334.6380* 📱 *lilleyslanding.com)*, **Ozark Mountain Guide Service** *(1933 Swallow Ln, Aurora* ☎ *417.337.1697*

☎ *tablerockguides.com*), **River Run Outfitters** *(2626 Hwy 165* ☎ *417.332.0460* ☎ *riverrunoutfitters.com*), **Rick's Chauffeured Guide Service** *(3322 S. Kimbrough Ave., Springfield* ☎ *417.861.3899* ☎ *bassguidepro.com*), **Scotty's Trout Dock and Marina** *(400 South Boxcar Willie Dr.* ☎ *417.334.4288* ☎ *scottystroutdock.com*), **State Park Marina** *(380 State Park Marina Rd.* ☎ *417.334.2628* ☎ *boatbranson.com*), **Taneycomo Fly Guide Service** *(140 Elizabeth Dr.* ☎ *417.699.3593* ☎ *taneycomofly.com*), and **White River Outfitters** *(738 Ozark Hollow Rd., Blue Eye* ☎ *417.779.1556* ☎ *whiteriveroutfitters.com*).

Outdoor Recreation

Outdoor enthusiasts are not disappointed when visiting the Ozarks. Wilderness, wildlife, and water are in abundance. Explore on foot, on horseback or by boat. Forget the hotel and pitch a tent under the stars.

DOGWOOD CANYON ✪ Must See!
(2038 W. Hwy 86, Lampe ☎ 417.779.5983

🖰 **dogwoodcanyon.com)** This breathtaking nature park is just a short drive south from Branson. For anyone visiting the area in spring or fall (especially around mid-October), a visit here is highly recommended. Make sure there are plenty of batteries in the camera. With over 2,200 acres of natural rock bluffs, waterfalls, streams, and other splendid scenery, Dogwood Canyon has a photo waiting to be taken at every turn.

A two-hour tram ride through the privately operated park is a worthy investment to learn about the canyon's history. There are several caves, some of which were used as Indian burial sites. The oldest human remains found in Missouri were inside one of the caves, dating back to 6,000 B.C. Among tour stops are the waterfall spot called Glory Hole and the Wilderness Church, which many brides have chosen as their wedding backdrop. The tour dips into Arkansas for an up-close look at buffalo, elk, and longhorn cattle. Reservations are strongly recommended for the canyon tour.

Other ways to explore Dogwood Canyon are by hiking its many nature trails, biking, guided horseback riding and even taking a Segway tour. Bikes and bike trailers are available to rent. Streams in Dogwood Canyon are stocked with brown and rainbow trout, and enthusiasts can fish alone or with a guide. (No license is required.) There is even a two-day Orvis fly-fishing school available by appointment. Call ☎ 800.235.9763 for more information on the school.

There is a small cafe in the park which offers lunch and snack items and a larger area is available to rent for groups. There are even log cabin accommodations. There is a charge for all activities. An adventure pass is available for those wanting to experience a variety of offerings. Call or go online for current prices. ($-$$$)

HIKING

The Branson area has beautiful hiking trails, both paved and natural terrain. Hike near the water or in the woods. There are trails of various lengths appealing to every level of ability.

LAKESIDE WILDERNESS HIKING TRAILS

It's hard to believe how close these trails are to the Branson Strip. It feels as if you are a million miles from civilization. In fact, you're behind Dick Clark's American Bandstand Theatre. The trails are part of the Lakeside Forest Wilderness, a 130-acre designated wilderness area maintained by the city of Branson. Park at the trailhead located off Fall Creek Road just behind the American Bandstand Theater.

The first trail, a mile in length round-trip, begins with level terrain and beautiful scenery. This portion of the trail is suitable for all ages and abilities. There is a deck overlooking Lake Taneycomo. The trail then becomes quite challenging with more than 300 stone steps leading toward a natural waterfall called Owen's Falls. The steep steps were built by Dr. Lyle Owen in the 1930s and require good walking shoes.

The second trail is 1 3/10 mile and offers a more leisurely walk. There is a picnic area at about the half-way point. The scenery here is always changing depending on the season and which of the many plants and trees are blooming.

TABLE ROCK STATE PARK TRAILS
(5272 Highway 165 ☎ 417.334.4704
🖥 mostateparks.com/tablerock.htm) Table Rock State Park's White River Valley Trail is the first to be designated for mountain biking in this area. Also popular with hikers, it is a brand new trail which has earned top honors nationally. It's more than ten miles of natural surface trail meanders through old homestead ruins and relics of the original Table Rock Dam construction.

The park is also home to the Table Rock Lakeshore Trail, 2.2 miles of paved pathway along the lake's shore. It's suitable for all ages and is a nice place for biking and rollerblading, too. Also at the park is the Chinquapin trail. It is about a mile in length and is a natural surface trail.

HORSEBACK RIDING

Experience the Ozarks the way people who lived here a hundred years ago did: on horseback. There are plenty of opportunities to take a trail ride through the woods. Each business has certain age, height and weight guidelines. Call for specific requirements. $=less expensive; $$=more expensive; $$$=most expensive.

BEAR CREEK TRAIL RIDES

(3400 Highway 65, Walnut Shade ● bearcreektrailrides.com)
Located seven miles north on Highway 65 this is an affordable one-hour trail ride. It meanders through shaded woods and returns along Bear Creek. A longer, two-hour trail ride is available for experienced riders. Bear Creek Trail Rides is open March through October and other times by appointment. ($)

DOGWOOD CANYON

(2038 W Hwy 86, Lampe ☎ 417.779.5983
● dogwoodcanyon.com) This is for guided horseback trail riding only. Guests are escorted three miles to the stables where they leave on a one-hour ride. Kids must be at least ten years old for this trail ride but, during the summer months there is a 15-minute junior trail ride offered for kids ages 3-9. ($$$)

SHEPHERD OF THE HILLS

(5586 W Hwy 76 ☎ 417.334.4191 ● oldmatt.com) Spend a half-hour trail ride on horses used in the Shepherd of the Hills Outdoor Drama. Ride on the "Trail Nobody Knows How Old" known from the infamous book by Harold Bell Wright. See other historic sites including the homestead where Wright experienced the Ozarks for the first time. Rides are available between Memorial Day and Labor Day. Must be seven years or older, a minimum of four feet tall and no more than 250 pounds. $$

UNCLE IKES

(8393 W Hwy 76, Notch ☎ 417.338.8449
● uncleikestrailride.com) Uncle Ike is taken from the character in Harold Bell Wright's book, The Shepherd of the Hills. Uncle

Ike was based on the real life postmaster, Levi Morrill. Located in the same area as the post office Morrill ran, Uncle Ike's Trail Ride offers guests the opportunity to ride trails dating back to the 1800's.

There are daily rides available from memorial to labor day as well as "meal" rides. Hot breakfast on the trail is offered for groups of 12 or more while dinner rides require just eight people. Specialty rides can also be arranged for romantic occasions or birthdays. Smaller children may be allowed to ride with an adult on certain trail rides. Call for reservations and special requests. ($$-$$$)

TABLE ROCK STATE PARK
(5272 Hwy 165 ☎ 417.334.4704

☗ mostateparks.com/tabletock.htm) Table Rock State Park recently won (by almost a two-to-one margin) the distinction of being the best state park in the Midwest in *AAA Midwest Magazine*. Developed in 1958 with the creation of Table Rock Dam the park has a myriad of outdoor recreation opportunities. There are more than 150 campsites, several trails for biking or walking and a large marina where nearly every kind of boat imaginable can be rented. The 48-foot sailing catamaran, Spirit of America, has scheduled cruises of the lake and even a water world adventure cruise which allows time for water play. The catamaran can also be chartered. The marina offers scuba gear and lessons and even parasailing. During the summer months a snack bar is open for business.

There are 22 picnic sites at the park and an open shelter which can accommodate 80-100 people. This area can be reserved for a fee or it can be used free of charge on a first come first served basis. While the park is on Table Rock Lake it is only a mile from Lake Taneycomo offering fishermen access to the best of both worlds.

CAMPING

Branson has an almost infinite number of camping facilities. It is home to some of the country's top spots for RVers as well as popular campgrounds for the tent camping crowd.

Camping can be extremely inexpensive or very pricey depending on the type of experience. Many of these campgrounds have a wide range of prices as they may offer basic tent sites, full hook-up RV sites and even top of the line cabins. Prices are categorized $=less expensive; $$=more expensive; $$$=most expensive.

ABC CAMPGROUND
(499 Buena Vista Rd. ☎ 417.336.4399 ☷ abc-branson.com)
There's a lot to appreciate at ABC Campground, but what stands out most is its owners, Jim and Sue Alkire. Guests feel like friends in a matter of minutes, and the couple is ready to help with any situation. It's no wonder this has consistently been voted the most RV-Friendly Good Sam Park in the nation. There are 160 sites here, with 136 pull-thrus. Sites can accommodate up to 45-foot motor homes. Six camping cabins are also available, along with three deluxe cabins that can accommodate up to six people comfortably. Pets are welcome.

The Celebrity Station Pavilion is definitely the center of town here and can be reserved free of charge. Facilities also include an outdoor pool and hot tub, a game room, and a playground with basketball, horseshoes, and badminton. Breakfast is available at the Pavilion each morning, often with live entertainment. There are several choices depending on appetite and budget. Various appetizer and dessert options are available for group gatherings. ABC offers special events for its guests on holidays. ($$-$$$)

BRANSON KOA CAMPGROUND
(397 Animal Safari Rd. ☎ 417.334.4414 🌐 bransonkoa.com)
Visitors to the Branson KOA Campground and Convention Center are enjoying a new location less than a mile from the Strip. There are tent camping sites, a variety of rental units, and 150 RV accommodations, from full-hookup 50-amp sites to water and electric–only sites, basic back-in and pull-thru sites, and premium and luxury sites. Luxury accommodations feature paved patios, private fireplaces, and patio furniture. Pets are welcome. In fact, there's a dog park called Kamp K-9 where they can experience their own vacation.

During peak season the campground offers breakfast and shuttle service. There's also pizza, ice cream, and homemade fudge. Kids can try the "Jumping Pillow," a cross between a trampoline and a bounce house. (The adults can jump, too.) Other facilities include a 7,000-square-foot convention center with a movable barbecue pit and conference seating for 600. ($$-$$$)

COOPER CREEK RESORT CABINS AND CAMPGROUND
(471 Cooper Creek Rd. ☎ 417.334.4871
🌐 coopercreekresort.com) Located on the shore of Lake Taneycomo just a couple of miles from Branson, Cooper Creek is rated in the top 3% of parks by Trailer Life. In addi-

tion to its 75 full hook-up sites there are more than twenty two-and-three bedroom cabins available for rent.

Fishing, a few boat rentals and a dock for guests, a convenience store, playground, laundromat and two swimming pools make this a nice choice for campers. Pets are also welcome for a small fee. ($-$$$)

INDIAN POINT
(3125 Indian Point Rd. ☎ 417.338.2121 🖰 recreation.gov)
Located just two miles from Silver Dollar City on Table Rock Lake this campground has 78 sites, the majority are equipped with electric and water. A swimming area, public marina, boat launch, group shelter and playground are among the amenities. Restrooms and showers are also available. ($)

LONG CREEK
(1036 Long Creek Rd., Ridgedale ☎ 417.334.8427
🖰 **recreation.gov)** Just south of Branson off Highway 86, this campground is located on Table Rock Lake. Run by the Corp of Engineers, there are 47 campsites here, some with electric or electric and water hookups. Showers and flush toilets are available. Amenities include a playground, marina, boat launch ramp and picnic areas. There is a two-night minimum stay. ($)

MILL CREEK
(1236 State Highway RB, Lampe ☎ 417.779.5378
🖰 **recreation.gov)** This campground is just west of Branson near Highway 13. All of its 67 campsites have electric and water hookups. Active families will love the volleyball and basketball courts, playground and opportunities to swim, boat and fish

in Table Rock lake. Restrooms with showers are available. A group shelter is also on site. Reservations must be made two days in advance and a two-night minimum stay is required. ($-$$)

PORT OF KIMBERLING RESORT

(49 Lake Rd., Kimberling City ☎ 417.739.2315 📞 mypok.com)
Nearly every type of vacation experience is available at this full-service, family owned resort. The retail area features "What's Up Dock," with a convenience store, Coyote's floating restaurant and the largest gas dock in the area. Everything from wake boards to house boats can be rented here. Ten other businesses near What's Up Dock make it the place to go for anyone looking to rent, buy, store, fill up or even clean a boat. The marina's day use area offers a picnic area, pavilion, boat launch and swim area for a small daily or annual fee.

The marina is home to every kind of traveler. The Port of Kimberling Suites offers hotel rooms. Not far from the hotel is a nice tent-camping area with a beach and swimming area, hiking trail, pavilions and even a playground for younger kids. The resort also offers RV hookups and cabins. The RV parking is near the cabins making it a nice option for multiple families. Cabins are equipped with full kitchens, decks, small barbeques, fireplaces and fire pits. The lofts are perfect (and fun) for kids but be aware the ceilings are low and beds are merely mattresses on the floor. The cabin bedrooms feature king or queen beds. Not far away are volleyball, basketball and tennis courts along with a baseball field. Nearby grocery stores make stocking up on supplies convenient. ($$)

TABLE ROCK STATE PARK

(5272 Hwy 165 ☎ 417.334.4704

⬤ **mostateparks.com/tablerock.htm)** There are 162 sites located on two campgrounds at Table Rock State Park. Both are equipped with modern shower houses and laundry facilities. One of the campgrounds is open year-round. Basic, electric and sewer/electric/water campsites are available. About two-thirds of the campsites can be reserved. A two-night minimum stay is required on weekends during the March–November season. Gates close every night at 10 p.m. ($-$$)

THE WILDERNESS LOG CABINS AND CAMPGROUND

(5125 Hwy 265 ☎ 800.477.5164 ⬤ thewildernesslogcabins.com) The 132 sites at this campground near Silver Dollar City are secluded and comfortable, with a foot of pea gravel to ease set-up and sleep. The three nearby bathrooms are absolutely spotless, with private showers. RV sites are available, along with RV rentals. Those looking for an old-fashioned family camping experience can check out the website for games and spooky campfire stories.

There are three playgrounds, a swimming pool, and a game room on the property. A shuttle transports campers to Silver Dollar City. ($-$$$)

GOLFING

Branson is quickly becoming one of the nation's top golf destinations, recognized by national publications like Golf Digest and Golfweek. Tom Fazio and Jack Nicklaus are among the names to have had a hand in designing courses here. The beautiful Ozark landscape, nice weather, and world-class courses draw some of the sport's top players—and many of Branson's top performers. Andy Williams, Mickey Gilley, Shoji Tabuchi, and others often can be found playing at their favorite courses.

Many of the courses are open all year, with reduced fees in the winter months. Groups and tournaments are welcome. Superior lodging is available on or near most courses. For information about courses and more, visit ● golfbranson.com.

BRANSON CREEK

**(1001 Branson Creek Blvd., Hollister ☎ 417.339.4653
● bransoncreekgolf.com)** *Golf Digest* and *Golf Magazine* have consistently given Branson Creek its #1 Public Course rating in Missouri, and the course has also held a *Golf Digest* top 100 spot. Designed by Tom Fazio, Branson Creek is a 7,000-yard course that features a par 71 championship layout with five sets of tees.

Branson Creek is located just a few miles south of Branson in Hollister. It offers private and group lessons, the largest practice facility in the area, and both a snack bar and a beverage cart (capable of catering for groups). No denim is allowed, and collared shirts and non-metal spikes must be worn. A 30-day advance tee time reservation is requested. ($$$)

DON GARDNER PAR 3 GOLF COURSE

**(201 Compton Dr. ☎ 417.337.8510
● bransonparksandrecreation.com/golf.htm)** This is an inexpensive, city-run course next to the Branson Community Center. Named after local golf professional Dan Gardner, it is a 9-hole, par 3 walking course suitable for all ages. There are two

Outdoor Recreation *(side tab)*

Outdoor Recreation   **207**

ponds, sand traps, trees, and bunkers to test skills; tee-to-hold distances range from 82 to 182 yards. A practice green is also available. No reservations are required. ($)

TOP OF THE ROCK GOLF COURSE

(Big Cedar Lodge, 612 Devils Pool Rd., Ridgedale ☎ 417.339.5200 📱 big-cedar.com) This 9-hole Jack Nicklaus signature golf course, featuring the superb views for which Big Cedar Lodge is known, is one of fewer than a dozen in the nation to be recognized as an Audubon Signature Cooperative Sanctuary Program golf course. The course and the Top of the Rock Restaurant are personal projects of Johnny Morris, owner of Bass Pro Shops and Big Cedar Lodge. ($$$)

LEDGESTONE

(1600 Ledgestone Way, Branson West ☎ 417.335.8187 📱 ledgestonegolf.com) Built in 1994, this course is a nice option for players of all levels. Some say it's the most scenic in the area, with its plush greens, mountain views, winding paths, and stream running through the course. Occasionally golfers see deer, turkey, and beavers. *Golf Digest* has called LedgeStone a "masterpiece of mountain golf architecture." There are 18 holes, with a challenging water feature.

The course looks intimidating because of its elevation but is less difficult than it appears. The front 9 is more open and flat, the back 9 tighter, with more trees. Each hole has a name, with a description and tips for playing it. LedgeStone also offers a driving range, a putting green, short game and bunker practice area. A number of tournaments are held here every year, including the Ironman during the coldest time of the year. The

Invitational is held the third week in August, during the hottest days of the year.

LedgeStone Grille is a casual restaurant in the clubhouse that serves soups, salads, appetizers, sandwiches, and pizzas. Upstairs is the restaurant, Steve's Treehouse. ($$$)

PAYNE STEWART GOLF CLUB
(100 Payne Stewart Dr. ☎ 417.337.2963
☷ paynestewartgolfclub.com) This course near Branson Landing is a tribute to Missouri native and professional golfer Payne Stewart, who died in a plane accident in 1999 at the age of 42. The well-liked golfer was known for his iconic style of knickers and tam-o'-shanter cap as well as his golfing skill. In his short life he won 11 tour events. Stewart is remembered at every tee box with a plaque telling a story about him.

The Payne Stewart course has been honored with titles like "Best New Course in America" and has been listed among the top five public access courses in Missouri by *Golfweek* magazine. This is considered by some to be the most challenging of Branson's courses, thanks to its many elevation changes, water features, trees, and other hazards.

Payne Stewart Golf Club has packages that include lodging. The Many Faces of Payne restaurant serves an upscale menu in a casual yet elegant atmosphere. It opens for breakfast and continues through early dinner. ($$$)

POINT ROYALE
(142 Club House Dr. ☎ 417.334.4477 ☷ pointroyalegolf.com)
Branson's original championship course, Point Royale is a

newly renovated, picturesque 18-hole, par 70 course. Those looking for a challenge will appreciate the bunkers on every hole. There are eight water holes and a water feature on the 12th hole.

This is a tight course with a lot of hills. Point Royale runs through the community, so there are houses on one side of most fairways, adding to the challenge. Point Royale is home to some of Branson's best-known names, including Andy Williams and Buck Trent. It's not uncommon to see the stars practicing their swings before a show. ($$)

MURDER ROCK

(Golf Club Dr., Hollister ☎ 417.332.3259 🌐 murderrock.com)
Murder Rock is a new course near Branson's airport, but its name and the site carry legends of lost treasure, murder, and even ghosts. Back in Civil War days, a bushwhacker named Alfred Bolin and his gang hid out at Murder Rock, and rumor has it that they murdered 20 people before Bolin himself was killed by a Union soldier. He was later beheaded and buried in an unmarked grave near Forsyth. Tales remain of a headless ghost watching over stolen treasure hidden somewhere at Murder Rock.

This violent history notwithstanding, golfers at Murder Rock enjoy its player-friendly course, named #25 among new courses by *Golf Week* and one of the top 50 courses for women by *Golf Digest*. The course was built by Landmark Land Company, which also designed and built Oaktree in Edmund, Oklahoma, and La Quinta in Palm Beach. The front 9 is actually 300 feet below the back 9, which gives the sense of playing on two different courses. Golf carts are equipped with GPS devices to keep everyone on track.

The views are spectacular. The clubhouse is built on the highest point in the county, and large windows in the restaurant take advantage of the setting. In warm weather guests can sit outside on the patio. The restaurant offers a nice ambiance, with cloth-covered tables, but serves casual fare like burgers, sandwiches, and soup. The hand-cut potato chips and salmon BLTs are favorites. ($$)

HOLIDAY HILLS

(2380 E Hwy 76 ☎ 417.334.4838 ⬤ holidayhills.com) Golfers have been playing at Holiday Hills for more than 70 years. Originally built in 1938, it was completely redone in 1997 to appeal to every level of golfer. The terrain is flatter than at many area courses, making it the most player-friendly. It has wide-open fairways and four tee boxes.

Holiday Hills is a par 68 course with more than 40 bunkers and water play on six holes. Golf carts are equipped with GPS devices. There is a restaurant, a lounge, and a fully stocked pro shop. This is a fairly inexpensive course compared to others in the area, giving golfers good value for the investment. ($)

THOUSAND HILLS GOLF AND CONFERENCE RESORT

(245 South Wildwood Dr. ☎ 417.336.5873 ⬤ thousandhills.com) Located right in the heart of Branson, this is a convenient course for many tourists. It's a par 64 course, so there are more par 3 holes than normal. That, according to country legend Mickey Gilley, makes Thousand Hills the perfect place to score your first hole in one. Still, this is a complex course with a lot of elevation changes. It's narrow in certain points, more open in others. Because Thousand Hills is set in a little valley, players must walk 30 steps or so down the side of a small hill to get from their carts to some holes.

Wildwood Creek runs through the course, adding a scenic waterfall. In addition, there are dramatic elevation changes and plenty of sand traps to challenge golfers. Designed by Robert E. Cupp, Thousand Hills is suitable for every level of player. GPS-guided carts give the distance to the greens. Restrooms along the course are pristine, with marble countertops and modern light fixtures.

Thousand Hills has three banquet rooms. Many choose this resort for weddings, family reunions, or corporate meetings. In addition, Thousand Hills offers condominium rentals on the course and cabins a short drive away. ($$)

TERRY'S TRANSPORT, TICKETS & GOLF
(190 Potential Dr., Hollister ☎ 417.331.2582 ⬢ ttbranson.com)
Terry Bowling is a seasoned golf professional who offers weekly outings to players of every skill level. Included are breakfast at Sadie's Sideboard & Smokehouse and 18 holes of golf, with advice from Terry to help improve your game. Games are played at the Holiday Hills or Thousand Hills course. Shuttle service is provided from select locations. Outings are seasonal from spring through fall.

Index

Index